John Langtry

Catholic Versus Roman

John Langtry

Catholic Versus Roman

ISBN/EAN: 9783744664226

Printed in Europe, USA, Canada, Australia, Japan

Cover: Foto ©Lupo / pixelio.de

More available books at **www.hansebooks.com**

CATHOLIC versus ROMAN;

OR,

SOME OF THE FUNDAMENTAL POINTS OF DIFFERENCE BETWEEN THE CATHOLIC CHURCH AND THE ROMAN CHURCH.

IN

TEN LECTURES,

DELIVERED IN ST. LUKE'S CHURCH, TORONTO, IN 1885.

BY

REV. J. LANGTRY, M.A.
RECTOR OF ST. LUKE'S.

TORONTO:
HUNTER, ROSE & COMPANY.
1886.

PRINTED AND BOUND BY
HUNTER, ROSE & CO.,
TORONTO.

PREFACE.

THE ten lectures contained in this book were called forth, as is explained in Lecture I., by an unprovoked and very misleading attack made by Archbishop Lynch in a lecture entitled, "The Difference Between the Catholic Religion and the Protestant Religions," which was published in the Toronto papers on September the 28th, 1885.

There is nothing new in that lecture. For fifteen years past the archbishop, or some of his fellow-workers have made precisely similar attacks at frequently recurring intervals. There has been nothing either in the public press, or the circumstances of the times to account for this. They have been altogether gratuitous and unprovoked attacks. They have contained the same perversions of history, the same misrepresentations of facts, and the same grossly insulting remarks and insinuations about the English Church as the offspiring of Henry the VIII.'s adulteries, or as the creation of the English Parliament.

For many years past, no one of these charges has been allowed to pass unchallenged; and in every instance where the press has allowed full and free discussion, the Archbishop and his satellites have been driven off the field—their charges disproved, their perversion of facts and Fathers brought home to them, and the truth vindicated to the no small discredit of the Roman communion.

This has, however, made no difference in their policy. Defeated and driven out of the public press—their own chosen field, they have had recourse to their own private religious papers, or have remained silent only till they have thought that their former discomfiture was forgotten, and then have issued forth again, repeating the same misrepresentations and calumnies, as though they had never been disproved. It may be that this course has been pursued for the purpose of reassuring the faltering faith of their own people, or it may be that they have learned by long experience the power over many minds of positive and oft-repeated assertion.

I have assumed in these lectures that the Archbishop has been sinning against light and knowledge in his misrepresentations of the position and history of the Church of England, but I have been told that that is not the most charitable construction to put upon his Grace's conduct. That a truer explanation is to be found in the fact that no Roman Catholic, clerical or lay, is allowed to have recourse to the original sources of knowledge; that they have no acquaintance with the actual facts of history, and no knowledge of patristic theology or testimony, except such as may be obtained through cooked compendiums and corrupted texts, and that the misrepresentations and calumnies which they are forever repeating have been so ingrained into their minds that, however, disproved, they cannot but believe them true. However this may be, they profess to be immensely surprised that any one should see anything insulting in their gross insinuations, misrepresentations and perversions of history.

With deliberate policy, and in the teeth of the palpable facts of the Church's history they assume with unhesitating persistency that the Roman Church is the Catholic Church, and as that was the name given from the very earliest times to the church which Jesus Our Lord founded, to which He gave His promises, and which He constituted as the temple and dwelling place of His Holy Spirit, they seek by repeated assertions to impress upon the public the conviction that all the powers and privileges of that original Catholic and Apostolic Church have descended to them alone. That whatever rights or gifts that historic church which Jesus founded may be proved to possess, can be found nowhere but in the Roman communion. It is a suicidal, but almost universal custom among non-Roman Christians to concede this arrogant claim, and to speak of the Roman Church as the Catholic Church, and of Romanists as Catholics. Catholics they are not, except in the one point of the historical continuity of the Roman Church, but in constitution, in doctrine, in spirit, and in practice they have departed

toto cœlo from the Catholic Church of the first ages. And
we are doing a positive and serious injury to the Church
of Jesus Christ in conceding that honourable, early, and
evangelical designation, to what can only be properly designated as Papalism or Romanism. Roman Catholics
profess to feel greatly insulted by being called Papists or
Romanists, but it is only because such a designation is a
repudiation of their claims to be Catholics. They are
not very particular about the insults they heap upon us.
And there is no reason why a true nomenclature should
be departed from, because it suits their pretensions to see
insult in its use. At all events, if they are to be spoken
of as Catholics at all, it ought never to be done without
the addition of the distinguishing adjective Roman,
which the Council of Trent has formally adopted as
their proper and legal designation.

At one of the April sessions of the Vatican Council
the bishops were in hot debate about the title of their
church. In the Schema it was called *Romana Catholica
Ecclesia.* Several desired the removal of the limiting adjective *Romana.* Among them an English bishop, who
told them that in his diocese land had been left by will
to the Catholic Church, and the Anglicans had appropriated it, on the ground that they were the Catholic
Church, and that the proper legal designation of his
church was Roman Catholic. In spite, however, of his,
and other protests the majority clung to the word Roman, which is now by the voice of infallibility proclaimed as their proper title.

The lectures were undertaken, as I have stated, at the request of laymen. I had no intention at first of occupying all the ground which they cover, and thought three lectures at most would dispose of the points which the Archbishop had raised. The extension to ten forced itself upon me by a logical sequence. I have in consequence been all along constrained for time, and have treated many points with meagre brevity, and all with a mechanical baldness of statement, which would probably have been avoided had I not been striving to condense and finish as speedily as possible.

It will be seen from this, that I have had no thought of taking up the whole Roman controversy. I have merely discussed the central and fundamental departures of the Roman Church from Catholic faith and practice.

The first four lectures were published in the *Mail* at the time of their delivery. When that journal closed its columns the *Orange Sentinel* and the *Dominion Churchman* continued the publication of the eight lectures that were delivered. Two lectures in this volume, that on the Inquisition, and that on Further Departures of the Roman Church from Catholic doctrines were not delivered and have not been published before. I had no intention of any publication, beyond that which the newspapers spontaneously undertook, but I have had so many solicitations from all parts of Canada and the United States to give the lectures to the public in a book or pamphlet form, that after long delay, I have determined to yield to a very widely expressed desire.

If they shall serve in any measure to dispel the delu-
sions which Rome is ever practising, to open people's eyes
to the actual facts of the case, and to win them to an intelligent acceptance of the truth, I shall be more than re-
paid for the no little toil which the preparation of even
so small a volume as this entails.

J. L.

LECTURE I.

THE CATHOLIC CHURCH: HER CONSTITUTION AND MODES OF ACTION.

Walk about Zion, and •go round about her ; tell the towers thereof.

Mark ye well her bulwarks, consider her palaces ; that ye may tell it to the generation following.—Ps. xlviii., 12, 13.

BY Zion is meant the Church of the living God. The text calls God's people to examine her structure, to consider carefully her principles, to see that they have a right knowledge of her strength and spaciousness as a safe and ample dwelling-place for His people, and to transmit, to the generations to come, a true conception, and accurate knowledge of those characteristic features by which she may be known. I do not intend to say more in the way of exposition of the text, or of its application to the subject I am about to treat. That will become apparent to your own minds as we proceed. The subject, you will remember, as I announced last Sunday evening, is the difference between the Catholic Church and the Roman Church. I told you that I had been impelled to take up this subject by the covert and utterly misleading attack, of Archbishop Lynch, upon the Church of England, in his lecture lately published in the papers.

I only wish to say, before proceeding, that in the now more than thirty years that I have been in the ministry I have never, to the best of my recollection, directly or indirectly assailed, in the pulpit, the belief or practice of any body of professing Christians. And although I was very indignant when I read this fresh and unprovoked assault, I should not have gone into this discussion, had I not been entreated by instructed and intelligent laymen, not to allow, what they characterized as this ignorant and insolent assault to pass unrebuked.

In the lecture to which I refer it is assumed, as is usual with Roman controversialists, that the Roman Church is the Catholic Church; and all who do not obey the Church of Rome, that is the Pope of Rome, are huddled together under the general designation of Protestants, and sneeringly referred to as standing all upon precisely the same footing; as deriving their origin either from Henry VIII. or from some one who has lived since his time. The Archbishop knows that this is an utter perversion of the truth. As a necessary result of this, the lecture is somewhat confused; and I shall not attempt to correct its misleading statements in the order in which they occur, though I shall reply to most of them as these lectures proceed.

Following the Archbishop's lead, I shall take a wider scope, and call attention to some of the characteristic points of difference between the Catholic religion and the Roman religions—I say religions, for, in spite of the Archbishop's boasting about the peace and union of the Roman communion, I shall be able to show that there is more than one religion believed in and allowed in the Roman obedience.

But some one will say, Why bother about the Catholic Church ? What we want to hear is the difference between the Protestant Church and the Roman Church, and the reason for that difference. We don't believe in the Catholic Church, and we don't care what it teaches. All I can say is, that we do. And we solemnly profess that belief every time we meet for public worship. We earnestly pray for the good estate of the Catholic Church every day. We hold ourselves bound by its faith and practice. And what is more, we claim to be the Catholic Church of this Realm, and maintain that the Roman Church, in addition to its manifold heresies, is a schism and an intrusion in this land. But what, then, you say, is this Catholic Church of which you speak ? I will do my best to explain, and I must ask you to be patient this evening. Many of you will, no doubt, be disappointed. We shall not reach much that is polemical to-ntght. I shall have to occupy most of the time at my disposal with very elementary statements.

There is no subject about which men's minds, at the present day, are in such utter confusion as about the meaning of the simple word " Church." There are a multitude of meanings attached to that word, and I charge the ultimate origin of this uncertainty and confusion upon Rome. It is due to her distortion of the Divine ideal, her invasions of the divinely-constituted authority and order of the Catholic Church of the first days, that men, in the frenzy of an outraged reason and conscience, have not known what to think or believe. I shall not, however, occupy your time with a detailed consideration, of even a few of the most influential, of the theories that are held at the present time about the Church. I ask you just to take your Bibles in your hands and go with me in learning first from its pages, and then from the testimony of the immediately subsequent ages, what the Church of the New Testament—the true Church, the Catholic Church— really is. It is necessary that we should have this point clearly in our minds before we proceed to contrast it with the Roman Church.

It is evident, then, even to a casual reader of the New Testament, that our Lord Jesus Christ became incarnate not only to make an atonement for sin— not only to teach men the truth concerning God and themselves—not merely to leave them an example as to how human life ought to be lived, but that, in addition to this, He came to found a Church or kingdom, to be the instrument of conveying to men the benefits of His incarnation and death, to be the witness and keeper of His Word, the ground and pillar of His truth. I say a Church or kingdom—for there can be no question but that by the phrase kingdom of heaven, or kingdom of God, our Lord means His Church on earth. He Himself uses these terms as interchangeable or convertible terms in St. Matthew, xvi., 18, 19. Under this title the Church had already been foretold in Daniel's great prophecy of the Kingdom of the God of Heaven, which shall never be destroyed. Both the Baptist and our Lord proclaim the setting up of this kingdom as the immediate result of His coming.

Out of the 39 parables which He spoke, 19 are parables of the kingdom ; and it is evident beyond dispute that by the kingdom of Heaven in them He means the Church in its present imperfect and mixed condition. The propagation and reception of that kingdom is described in the parable of the sower ; its condition, as having bad people in it as well as good, in that of the tares and wheat ; its small beginning and rapid extension in that of the mustard seed ; the hidden transforming working of the Spirit of God in it, in that of the leaven. The net describes the intermingling of the good and bad in this kingdom of heaven even till the end. And, finally, that by this term he means the Church on earth is placed beyond discussion by the declaration that at the end of the world the angels shall gather out of His kingdom all things that offend and them that do iniquity. There are none that offend or do iniquity in the kingdom of glory ; no tares or bad fish mingle with the good there. The description can only apply to the present probation state of that kingdom, in which good and evil are forever commingled and forever struggling for the mastery.

But though the Lord usually speaks of the society which He was founding under the title of a kingdom, it is to Him that we owe the word by which in all times, from the Apostles downwards, it has been most usually called. Upon this rock, that is, of Peter's confession of his deity, as most of the Fathers interpret it, " I will build my Church, and the gates of hell shall not prevail against it." Again, He directs that an offending brother who refuses to listen to private admonition is to be reported to the Church ; but if he neglect to hear the Church he is to be treated as a heathen man and a publican. The word translated Church means a body called out of the general mass of the people. Just as Abraham and his seed were called out of the rest of mankind and formed into a separate Church, so individuals are called out of all nations and formed into a distinct Christian society This society is not made up of a number of people living in the world, merely holding Christian doctrine, and bound together in nothing but by a community of sentiment. They who belong to it are called out of the world, the kingdom of darkness, and translated into the kingdom of light (col. i., 13).

It is not an invisible, unorganized brotherhood made up of all good people. For it was organized into a kingdom by our Lord Himself, and He is its head and king. It has, moreover, its subordinate officers, its laws, its badges of authority, its oaths of allegiance, its mode of admission, its tests of loyalty, and it is invested with power to extend and perpetuate itself.

It is not an invisible company of true believers, for it is made up of good and bad members; some that offend and do iniquity, who will not, and cannot, be gathered out till the harvest, the end of the world, is come. If the Church described in the New Testament, which our Lord founded, and to which He gave His promises, be invisible, then clearly every visible thing on earth, calling itself a church, is not only unscriptural and wrong—but is guilty of fraud—of a wicked attempt on the part of a mere human society by appropriating a name which does not belong to it, to delude people into a notion that by joining it, they will secure to themselves the promises and privileges which belong to another society altogether.   It is the same sort of dishonesty as would be perpetrated by a new firm taking the name of an old and well-established house, in order to gain for itself the credit and custom that belong to the old and secure establishment.

The term Church is used more than a hundred times in the New Testament, and is never once used as the name of an invisible brotherhood, but always as the name of that visible organized body to which Christ himself applied it.   On the very day after His baptism He began to call His Church out and gather it around him.   Shortly afterwards He proceeded to organize it into a visible society by the appointment of the twelve apostles, whom He sent forth to proclaim, as He Himself had done, " The kingdom of heaven is at hand."   He appointed other seventy to aid them in their work.   He promised to be with them always, even unto the end of the world.   He declared, " As My Father hath sent Me even so send I you."   He assured them that they should be indued with power from on high to fit them for their work.   He invested them with authority to bind and to loose.   He appointed a definite outward form, Christian baptism, for admitting new members into his kingdom ; prescribed laws for their government when admitted, and laid down principles for the guidance of their life.   This Church thus called out and organized began its supernatural life, of the one spirit in the one body, against which the gates of hell shall not prevail, in the upper chamber in Jerusalem on the day of Pentecost.   The Lord had prepared it a body in the hundred and twenty who were gathered together at Jerusalem waiting the fulfilment of Christ's promise of the Comforter; and as the Holy Ghost breathed into Adam's body the breath of life, and he became a living soul, so the same Holy Ghost came upon the infant Church, filling it with supernatural life, and sending it forth on its great mission to evangelize the world. And everywhere they that gladly received the Word were baptized by the one Spirit into the one body.

This body is divine in its constitution, for Christ organized it. It is divine in its life, for the Holy Spirit dwells in it as its creator, incorporating it into Christ. It is declared to be the body of Christ. Christ Himself is the Head of the Church, which is His body. His Church is declared to be the bride of Christ; it is the Lamb's wife; figures which declare that she is joined to Him in the closest and most indissoluble union. And the voice of inspiration tells us that as there is only one Spirit, one Lord, one Faith, one Baptism, one God and Father of all, so there is *only one body* to which these high privileges and promises belong.

You can see, then, from your New Testament that the shallow boast of Roman Catholics that their Church was the first Church, the mother and mistress, therefore, of all Churches, is simply not true. The first church was the Church of Jerusalem, and all its members were Jews. From Jerusalem it extended to other places. First, Philip preached the truth in Samaria, and established a Church there by admitting his converts into the one body by baptism. Then the Gentile proselyte, the treasurer of Queen Candace, was admitted into this society in the

same way.   Then the Gentile Cornelius and his house-
hold.   The Church has spread until it embraces Jews,
Samaritans, proselytes, and Gentiles.   And still Jerusalem
is the centre of interest, the Mother Church of the
world.

After this the Sacred History tells us that the Church
was next established at Antioch, the great and luxurious capital of Syria; then in Cyprus.   Then Barnabas
and Saul, who had been separated for this special mission, passed over into Asia Minor and preached in
Pisidia, Antioch, Iconium, Lystra, and Derbe, ordaining
elders everywhere to take charge of the new churches.
Then in a second journey Paul and Silas passed west-
ward, through Galatia, founding new churches, until,
guided by a vision, they passed over into Macedonia,
the first apostolic heralds of the Gospel in Europe.
Gathering congregations and planting churches in Macedonia and Greece, at Phillippi, Thessalonica, Bærea,
Athens, and Corinth, they finally returned to Asia.
Then after two years' residence at Ephesus and two
years' imprisonment at Cæsarea St. Paul went as a
prisoner to Rome, more than twenty years after the
Church in Jerusalem was founded.   And it appears, from
Rom. xv., 21 and 22, that neither had he himself been
there before nor had any apostle preceded him.   He
found there a considerable community of Christians, who
had probably been brought to a knowledge of the truth
by the strangers of Rome at Jerusalem who were converted on the day of Pentecost.

And so we see, in ever-widening circles, either by
the ministry of the Apostles themselves or of those

whom they ordained in every city, the church was founded and congregations multiplied in one land after another, till the whole known world was permeated with this new leaven, filled with the spreading branches of this rapidly-developing mustard tree. Thus, while these things were transpiring, or at a very early date, missionaries from Ephesus founded flourishing churches in Gaul, at Marseilles and Lyons. And we read that when the first persecution fell upon them with devastating fury, vast numbers of Christians fled and hid themselves in the forests of the west. Large numbers, passing over the sea to the islands of Britain, sought refuge among their Celtic kinsmen in England and Scotland. And whether they were the first heralds of the Gospel there or not, they were at least, in all probability, the instruments by which the Gospel was made known in those parts of Britain that were inaccessible to Roman arms, where Tertullian, living in the next century, tells us there were vast numbers of Christians in his day.

During the apostolic days this body thus extended was everywhere designated by the one substantive word, the Church. It is called *the* Church more than seventy times in the Acts and the Epistles. After a time it was thought desirable to add the adjective Catholic —meaning universal, or for all—for the purpose of distinguishing the Church which was intended to extend into all lands and to embrace all peoples, from the Jewish Church, which was meant for one race and confined to one small corner of the earth. Before long this word Catholic took on, as is not uncommon in the history of language, a second meaning, and was used to distinguish . those who held the whole truth from the heretics who chose, as their name implies, parts of the truth as their creed. Another adjective, Apostolic, was added to the description of the Church, as in the Nicene Creed, to distinguish the Church which continued in union and communion with the Church which the Apostles founded and presided over, from those bodies which separated themselves and took the name of their founder or favorite doctrine. This Church also received local designations from the cities or countries in which it was established, as the Church of Jerusalem, of Samaria, of Egypt, of Rome, of Gaul, of England. Then in ordinary conversation the other distinguishing adjectives were dropped, and it was spoken of merely as the Church of Rome, of France, or of England, or more generally merely as the Church; everybody knowing that the body meant was the Catholic Apostolic Church of Gaul, Rome or England.

But everywhere it was the same body, organized in the same way, ruled by the same officers and general laws, animated by the one Spirit, preaching the one Gospel, professing the one Faith : the Church in one land owning and owing no subjection to the Church in another, but all co-operating in the one great effort to win the world to Christ. If difficulties arose or new doctrines were preached, they were either composed by the bishop or reported to a council like that in Jerusalem described in Acts xv. These councils were either diocesan, provincial, or general. To the provincial councils the bishops and clergy of the province were summoned. If the difficulties

were of sufficient importance, those of the whole Christian
world were summoned, that by their testimony the truth
might be settled and difficulties removed. Archbishop
Lynch says " there must be a visible head and chief
director, some man on earth to be the head ruler of His
Church on earth."   All I can say is that centuries passed
away before anybody discovered that necessity—or even
thought of it.   The Catholic Christians of those days
had no such easy method as Archbishop Lynch describes.
They had no supreme ruler and director to whom they
could appeal to teach them new doctrines or to define
old ones.   They had to summon the bishops and clergy
from all parts of the world, to undertake long and
perilous journeys : to come together to establish the truth
and quiet heresies.

And when they had assembled together in council,
what was their mode of proceeding ? Did they, as
Romanists assert, only assemble at the call of the Pope,
or by his permission ? Did they only deliberate under his presidency ? Did they patiently await and
meekly accept his announcement of new doctrines or
definition of old ones ? Not a bit of it. The Bishop
of Rome, unless all testimony deceives, no more called,
or was asked for his sanction to summon, one of those
six great general councils, which promulgated the creeds
and formulated the doctrines of the Church, than the
Bishop of London called or sanctioned them. He was not
present at any one of them. His expressed wish—nay,
his entreaty—as to where two of them were to be held,
was utterly disregarded and overriden. His Church was
hardly represented at all. His judgment was not asked

for or referred to; and yet he accepted, like the other bishops of the Christian world, not his decisions without the council, but the council's decisions without him. (See note A).

How, then, did these councils proceed in determining the truth? They did not proceed to settle the points in dispute by asking this bishop or that presbyter what his opinion about it was; but, setting the Scriptures upon a throne in their midst, as containing the truth of God, they collected the testimony of the Church, asking first one bishop or presbyter, and then another, as to the interpretation that had been handed down to them from the beginning with reference to the matter in dispute. Thus was the one faith once for all delivered, defined and confirmed while the interpretation of apostles and inspired men was still living and remembered in the Church. Such, my brethren, in brief outline, was the Catholic Church when the name Catholic was first given to her. Such her condition as she emerges through the dust and turmoil of her earliest encounter with an unbelieving world into the clear light of historic times. A spiritual kingdom owing obedience to her invisible Head and Lord, and yet herself visible—a vast organized democracy—her bishops in every diocese invested with the same authority and standing upon a footing of perfect spiritual equality;* her doctrines defined and defended, and her discipline settled by a church parliament representing the diocese, the province, or, when need arose, the whole world.

I shall show on Sunday evening next how the Roman Church has departed from this Apostolic ideal, and by

her doctrines of supremacy and infallibility has overturned the constitution of the Catholic Church. May
God restrain us from all passion, guide us into a clearer
knowledge of his truth, and a heartier obedience to His
will.

---

*This fact alone subverts the whole Roman theory of the Pope's supre-
macy and autocratic headship over the whole Church. That theory involves
the assertion which is freely made, that the Pope alone has authority to
summon or preside at a General Council of the whole Church. And so,
while it is undeniable that the Emperor Constantine summoned the first
General Council at Nice (A.D. 325), and that Hosius, Bishop of Cordova,
in Spain, presided at it, modern Roman controversialists assert, without
the shadow of authority from any cotemporary records for the assertion,
that the Emperor summoned the Council in obedience to the Pope's commands, and that Hosius attended and presided as his representative and
legate. Neither the records of the Council nor its Synodal epistle, nor any
of the cotemporary, or nearly cotemporary, historians, Eusebius, Socrates,
Sozomen or Theodoret give even a hint of the truth of these assertions.
There is no earlier authority for either of these statements than that of
Gelasius of Cyzicus, a writer of the fifth century, when the Bishops of
Rome were already setting up extravagant claims, and he, by common
consent of Roman Catholic writers, is an utterly untrustworthy witness.
The careful Dupin calls him a sorry compiler, who gathered all he met with
 . . . without examining whether it was true or false. Natalis Alexander condemns the work as overflowing with mistakes. Velenus rejects it
as "containing much spurious matter and falsehood." In proof of the un-
truth of the unsupported assertion of this fifth century writer, we have the
declaration of the historian Socrates [Bk. V., preface], that "the greatest
synods have been, and still are, convened by the determination and appointment of the Emperors," a declaration which is established by the fact that
though Pope Leo I. implored the Emperor Theodosius to summon a General
Council at Rome, the Emperor obstinately refused; and that when the
Emperor Marcian did summon the Council, he, too, utterly disregarded the
same Pope's request that it might be held in Italy, and summoned it, *solely
in the Emperor's own name*, to meet at Calcedon. In further confirmation
of the truth of this statement, we have the fact that in the prefaces to the
acts of the first six General Councils, reaching up to A.D. 680, no mention
is made of any other authority for summoning them than that of the Emperors.

But more than this, we have the Emperor's own declaration : " By the suggestion of God, *I summoned* to Nice most of the Bishops with whom . . . . I undertook the investigation of the truth.—Socrates I., 9.

Again, in the Synodal Letter of the Council, sent to absent Bishops and distant Churches, we read : " Since by the grace of God, and the favoured-of-God, King Constantine, collecting us from different cities and provinces, the great and holy Synod was celebrated at Nice.—Socrates I., 9.

Again, Socrates says (I., 8), " When therefore the Emperor beheld the Church unsettled, . . . he convoked a General Council, summoning all the Bishops to meet him at Nice."

Again, Sozomen says (I., 17), " Constantine called together a Synod at Nice, in Bithynia, and wrote to the superintendents of the Churches in every country, directing them to be there on an appointed day.'

Theodoret says of Constantine (I., 7), " He proceeded to summon the celebrated Council of Nice."

Epiphanius, who was 15 years old when the council of Nice was held, says (LXIX., 11, Heresies), " The Emperor, taking care for the Church, summoned the Œcumenical Synod of 318 Bishops, whose names are still preserved."

In a letter by the Emperor Justinian, read before the Second Council of Constantinople, A.D. 553, and approved by the Bishops, it is stated (Collat. I.), " Wherefore Constantine, of pious memory, when Arius was blaspheming, congregated at Nice, from different dioceses, 318 Fathers."—(Labbé, tom. V., col. 419.)

But not only did the Emperor summon the Council of Nice ; it was he who opened the solemn session of the Council. Constantine acted as honorary president at the first, and then ceded his place to the ecclesiastical president (Euseb., Vit. Const. III., 12, 13), and so Pope Stephen the V. speaks of the Emperor as having in fact presided at the Council of Nice (Hardouin V., 1119). With regard to the representatives of Rome we have the following testimony :

Socrates (I., 8) says, " The Prelate of the Imperial City was absent through age, but his presbyters were present and filled his place."

Sozomen (I., 17) and Eusebius (Vit. Const. III., 7) bear exactly the same testimony, and ·mention the names of the two presbyters who came as representatives of the aged Bishop of Rome.

Theodoret (I., 7) says " The Bishop of Rome sent two presbyters to the Council for the purpose of taking part in all the transactions."

After the withdrawal of the Emperor, his friend and counsellor, Hosius of Cordova, on whose advice he had summoned the Council, presided, and as president his name stands first in the signatures to the Nicene creed, as follows : " From Spain, Hosius, from the City of Cordova. I believe thus as it is written above."

The next signature is "Vito and Innocentius Priests. We have signed for our Bishop, who is Bishop of Rome. He believes thus as is written here." Hosius signed for himself, without a word about representing the Pope. The Pope's representatives sign for him, without a word about Hosius. Lastly, as regards the formal confirmation of the acts of the Council. This, too, was the work of Constantine alone, and no hint of the Pope having any authority or right to be consulted appears in the ancient records. It is the Emperor, too, who writes to the Bishops (the Pope among the rest) to enforce the decrees, to improve and erect churches, and to impose penalties for fostering Arianism [see his five letters in Socrates I., 9]; so that the whole story of the Pope summoning the Council through Constantine, and of Hosius presiding as his representative, is a manifest fiction, invented to support pretentions that had not been put forth till long after the Council of Nice was held.

The foregoing condensed evidence is extracted from the Rev. J. M. Davenport's pamphlet (Papal Infallibility, pages 96-97).

NOTE B, LECTURE I.

*It has been objected by a Roman Catholic writer that to describe the Church as a visible body without a visible head, is to represent it as a "monstrosity." But it has been well said in reply, that if this be a monstrosity St. Paul, and not Mr. Langtry, is responsible for it, since he says, "Christ is the Head of the Church, and the Saviour of the body;" and it has been pertinently asked, "would a body with two heads, one visible, the other invisible, be less of a monstrosity?" Pope Gregory I. has formally enunciated the very same doctrine, declaring "that Christ is the one only Head of the Church."

LECTURE II.

POINTS OF DIFFERENCE BETWEEN THE ROMAN CHURCH AND THE CATHOLIC CHURCH IN CONSTITUTION AND GOVERNMENT.

IN endeavouring, last Sunday evening, to follow out the duty here enjoined, of examining with unceasing care the structure, strength, and glory of the Church of God, we learned from the plain statements of God's own Word, and the earliest uninspired records concerning her, that the Catholic Church, when the name Catholic was first given to her, was a vast, visible, organized society ; or, if you prefer it, a constitutional monarchy, with its King in the mother city, Heaven ; with universal suffrage, and universal representation in those parliamentary councils by which her faith was formulated, her doctrines defined and her discipline regulated. That she knew of no supreme visible head, no man who was chief ruler and universal teacher, to whom she could go for instruction in doctrine and correction in morals and in discipline. That she proceeded in those councils to deliberate and legislate and define without the call or permission or presence of the Bishop of Rome, or any other particular bishop. That the

B

Bishop and Church of Rome, like all other bishops and churches of Christendom, accepted both the doctrinal and disciplinary decrees made, not by the Pope without the council, but by the council without the Pope. For instance, at the Second Œcumenical Council, in 381, which decreed the most important definition of faith since the Nicene, by first formulating the doctrine of the Holy Ghost, the Church of Rome was not represented at all; and the decrees were communicated to her just as they were to other Churches, and were accepted without opposition or demur. And so it went on for centuries. The Catholic Church knew of no other way of defining doctrines and settling disputes but by the testimony of the Church, through the agency of her councils.* "For the first thousand years of Church history not one question of doctrine was finally decided by the Pope. The Roman bishops took no part whatever in the discussions and deliberations which the numerous Gnostic sects, the Montanists and Chiliasts, produced in the early Church. Nor can a single doctrinal decree issued by one of them be found during the first four centuries, nor a trace of the existence of any. Even the fierce controversy about Christ, kindled by Paul of Samosata, which occupied the whole Eastern Church for a long time, and necessitated the assembling of several councils, diocesan and provincial, was carried on and terminated without the Pope taking any part in it whatever. So, again, in the chain of controversies connected with the names of Theodotus, Artemon,

---

* Bossuet, in his Notes on the Synodal letter of the Council of Constantinople, says: "From this it is clear that questions of faith are settled solely by the consent of the Churches.

Noetus, Sabellius, Berryllus, and Lucian of Antioch, which troubled the whole Church and extended over 150 years, there is no shred of proof that the Roman bishops acted beyond the limits of their own local Church, or accomplished any doctrinal result." (Janus).

There were three great controversies during this early period in which the Church of Rome did take part, viz., about Easter, about heretical baptism, and about the penitential discipline. But in all these the will and judgment of the Popes were rejected, and the other Churches maintained their own views and usages without its leading to any permanent division. Several African and Asiatic synods decided against the validity of schismatical baptism. Pope Stephen took the opposite view, and tried to compel these Churches into agreement with himself by excluding them from his communion; but it only drew down on him the sharp censure of St. Cyprian, of Carthage, and St. Firmilian, of Cæsarea, for his insolence in presuming to dictate doctrines to other Bishops and Churches; and the great St. Augustin justified and upheld them in their action.

In the great Arian controversy, which engaged and disturbed the Church above all others, and was discussed in more than fifty synods, the Roman See for a long time took no part. Popes Julius and Liberius (337-366) were the first to take part in this great struggle; but it was only to involve themselves in heresy, which the Church and subsequent Popes of Rome acknowledged and denounced. During the fourth century councils alone decided all dogmatic questions, and nobody else was thought of as having a right to do so. So well was this known that Pope Siri-

cius (384-398) declined to pronounce upon the false doctrine of a bishop, Borosus, when requested to do so, on
the ground that he had no right to do so, and must await
the sentence of the bishops of his Province. And so, when
Pope Vigilius first approved, and then, to please the emperor, condemned what is known as the three chapters,
and then in fear of the Western bishops again approved
them, the Fifth General Council excommunicated him ;
and he finally submitted to the judgment of the council,
declaring that he had been a tool in the hands of Satan.
Upon this whole national churches, those of Africa, North
Italy, and Illyria, held councils and excommunicated
the Pope, whom they denounced for having sacrificed the faith.

"Again, Pope Honorious was unanimously condemned
by the Sixth General Council as a heretic, for having
publicly sided with the Monothelite heresy, and offi-
cially taught it in dogmatic pontifical letters in reply
to a formal application from the Eastern Patriarchs to
him as Pope to declare his opinion. The legates of his
own successor, Pope Agatho, took the lead at that
council in anathematizing him ; and a successor of his,
Leo II., wrote to assure the Spanish bishops that Honorius and his acccomplices in heresy were certainly
damned. The seventh and eighth so-called General
Councils repeated the sentence, while every Pope for
several centuries had to renew the sentence at his cor-
onation, and declare his infallible predecessor a heretic."
(Littledale). (See note A at the end of this chapter).

So, again, the Western Church alone, on its own
authority, in its councils, deposed Popes John XII.,

Benedict IX., Gregory VI., Gregory XII., and John XXII. the last in express terms as simoniac, sorcerer and heretic. And these depositions by councils have been all along acknowledged as perfectly valid, and the Popes set up instead of the deposed ones as lawful tenants of the Roman chair, instead of being regarded as they would now have to be regarded, as blasphemous rebels against the vicar of God on earth, and the new Popes as schismatic intruders. It needs no arguments of mine to prove to the simplest mind that these facts establish beyond dispute : 1st. That the councils, and not the Popes, were up to this date known and recognized as the supreme legislative and governing bodies of the Church. 2nd. That the claim of Papal supremacy, if put forth, was utterly rejected and disregarded by the whole body of the Church ; and 3rd. That they flatly contradict and sweep out of existence the very possibility of Papal infallibility. For if Vigilius, Honorius and John XXII. fell into deadly heresy, where is the infallibility ?

The same inference follows from the Council of Verulum (St. Albans), A. D. 793, which was called without the consent of the Pope, and which denounced the image worship, to which the Pope had lately committed himself, as " a thing which the Church of God utterly abhors." And so the great Council of Frankfort, which assembled at the call of the Emperor Charlemagne in A. D. 794, and which was attended by large numbers of bishops from France, England, Germany and Italy, including the Pope's legates, and which in spite of their opposition, condemned as " execrable in the Church of God all worship, adoration and service of images," and this though they knew that the Pope had publicly committed himself to that worship and was urging upon them its enforcement upon Christians. And Pope Adrian did not venture to do more than offer a verbal opposition. Once more the bishops assembled at the great Synod of Paris in 824 did not hesitate when discussing this subject to denounce " the absurdities of Pope Adrian, who, they said, had commanded an heretical worship of images." So, again, when Charlemagne urged Pope Leo III. to accept the " *Filioque* " clause in the Nicene creed, which the Synod of Aix authorized, Leo replied that the doctrine was true, but that the decision of such questions belonged not to him but to an œcumenical council.

From what has been said we get the following picture of the organization of the Primitive Catholic Church : " Questions of primary importance or those affecting the whole Church, are settled by the Church Universal through her representatives in œcumenical council assembled. All other questions are settled on the spot either by the bishop of the diocese or by the bishop and his synod, or by the provincial or national synod ; for the Church is organized into dioceses, provinces, patriarchates, and, as the empire broke up and formed itself into the modern nations, into national Churches ; each of these manages its own affairs with perfect freedom and independence, and maintains its own traditional usages and discipline, subject only to the government of the whole Church. Laws and articles of faith of universal obligation are issued only by the whole Church concentrated into an œcumenical council." So thoroughly was this constitution enwrought into the texture of the Church's life, that for centuries after the Papal claims were put forth and formulated, and even widely accepted, the Church still proceeded to legislate through her councils and synods, often without the Pope's concurrence or permission being sought for, and often in direct opposition to his will and pronounced judgment. Even during those last dark days of Papal rule which preceded the Reformation movement, when, as Dr. Dollenger tells us, for two hundred and fifty years the whole of Europe was crying out for a reformation of the intolerable corruption of doctrine, discipline, and morals that was strangling the spiritual life of Europe, it was not to the Popes of Rome that anybody turned for help. The cry of Europe was for a free general council of the whole Church. To such a council Luther and his followers, to whom the notion of a permanent separation from the ancient Church had not occurred, made their appeal. To such a council the English Church offered to submit her dispute with Rome, binding herself to accept the result, because she was satisfied that the truth would be brought to light. And that appeal remains unrevoked to this day.

Such was the constitution of the Catholic Church in the beginning ; and, in spite of the prolonged struggles, for centuries after the name of Catholic was given to her. How does the Church of Rome of the present day correspond with this picture, or rather how widely does she differ from the primitive constitution and order of the Catholic Church ? This difference is briefly expressed in Cannons iii. and iv. of the Vatican Council, which bind all Roman Catholics now. Cannon iii. affirms, " If anyone shall say that the Roman Pontiff has

only the office of supervision and direction, but that
he has not plenary and supreme power of jurisdiction
over the whole Church, not only in things which pertain to faith and morals, but also in those which pertain
to the discipline and government of the Church spread
throughout the world, or that he has only greater parts
and not the whole plenitude of this supreme power, or
that this power is not ordinary and direct, or over all
and singular churches, or over all and singular pastors and
faithful, let him be anathema." A clause of Canon iv.
says :—" We teach and define as a divinely revealed
dogma that the Roman Pontiff when he speaks *ex cathedra*,
that is, when he is discharging the office of pastor and
teacher of all Christians, he defines by his supreme apostolic authority, through that divine assistance promised
in the Blessed Peter, a doctrine to be held by the whole
Church concerning faith or morals, he possesses that infallibility which the Divine Redeemer willed that His
Church should be intrusted with for defining doctrines
concerning faith and morals, so that these definitions of
the Roman Pontiff thus delivered are of themselves,and not
because of the consent of the Church, irreformable. If anyone presumes to contradict this our definition, let him be
anathema." The points are plain. The parliamentary councils are nowhere. The Pope has plenary and absolute
power of jurisdiction. He, and not the council, defines
the doctrines that are to be held by the whole Church,
not only in matters of faith and morals, but in matters
of government. And that these doctrines are irreformable, not because they express the consent and concurrence of the whole Church, but because they are delivered

by the Pope. The contradiction of primitive Catholic teaching on the subject of the definition, defence and promulgation of the faith—confirmed, as I have shown that teaching is, by more than one Pope—is direct and absolute. The overthrow of the Catholic organization and government of the Church is complete. The organized democracy, the constitutional monarchy, has been subverted, and an absolute autocracy, ruled with irresponsible and plenary power by one man has been substituted for it. To him all alike, layman and cleric, king and beggar, are equally and absolutely subject. The ancient office of the Church, to witness to and define and defend the truth, has been swept away. The Pope is the universal pastor and teacher of all Christians. He alone defines and declares the faith. He is the supreme head and governor of the whole Church. No one has any rights before him, and all authority in the Church and in the world is an emanation from his, a mere deputed power that may at any moment be recalled. The Church, according to Cardinal Cajetan, " is the slave of the Pope ; neither in its whole nor its parts (national Churches) can it desire, strive for, approve, or disapprove anything not in absolute accordance with the Papal will and pleasure." He, as Bellarmine has not feared to express it, is " vice-God ;" and the *Civilta*, the Papal organ, asserts that " all the treasures of divine revelation, of truth, righteousness, and the gifts of God are in the Pope's hand. He carries on Christ's work on earth, and is in relation to us what Christ would be if He were still visibly present to rule His Church. The Pope it calls " the summum oraculum—which can give at once an infallible solution of every doubt, speculative and practical." ·

A Roman Catholic writer of the liberal school, speaking in reference to this, says, when once the old notion of adhering to the organization and teaching of the ancient Church is broken through, the horror of new doctrines got rid of, and the well-known cannon of truth formulated by St. Vincent—"*quod semper, quod ubique, quod ab omnibus*"—is altogether set aside, then every Pope, however ignorant of theology, will be free to make what use he likes of his power of dogmatic creativeness, and to erect his own thoughts into the common belief binding on the whole church.   We say advisedly, however ignorant of theology, for the Jesuit theologians have already foreseen this contingency as being not an unusual one with Popes, and one of them, Professor Ebermann, of Mayence, has observed, " A thoroughly ignorant Pope may very well be infallible, for God has before now pointed out the right way by the mouth of a speaking ass."   And then he adds, "Whoever, after the adoption of infallibility as a dogma, dares to question the plenary authority of any new article of faith coined in the Vatican mint, will incur, according to the Jesuit interpretation, excommunication in this world, and everlasting damnation in the next. Councils will, in the future, be superfluous. The bishops will no doubt be assembled in Rome now and then to swell the pomp of a papal canonization, or some other grand ceremony ; but they will have nothing more to do with dogmas. If they wished to confirm a papal decision itself the result of direct divine inspiration, this would be bringing lanterns to aid the light of the noonday sun." (See note B at end of this chapter).

And yet, to prove the dogma of papal infallibility

from Church history, nothing less is required than a complete falsification of it. The declarations of popes which contradict the present doctrines of the Church of Rome, or contradict each other (as the same pope sometimes contradicts himself), have now to be twisted into agreement, so as to show that their mutually destructive enunciations are at bottom sound doctrine, and not really contradictory of one another. But they will not find much difficulty here. The creatures of the Papacy, and especially the Jesuits, never had any particular difficulty in manufacturing church history. They have performed most incredible feats in this line. They have forged, and falsified and invented until no ordinary Roman Catholic, priest or layman, has any true notion of the facts of the past. The whole fabric of papal supremacy and infallibility is built upon a foundation of the most bare-faced forgeries and lies. But no forgeries or inventions will help them to explain to the common sense of mankind this strange phenomonon : " That a dogma which requires us to believe, on the pain of damnation, that Christ, from the beginning of the Gospel, made the Pope of the day the one vehicle of his inspirations, the pillar and exclusive organ of Divine truth, without whom the Church is like a body without a soul, deprived of the power of vision, and unable to determine any point of faith ; that this dogma which is now the primary article of the faith, the keystone of the whole Roman system of doctrine and practice, was not certainly ascertained to be true until the year of grace 1869 " ; nay, that it was so far from being believed to be true that Keenan's controversial catechism, endorsed by the whole Irish episcopate,

formally approved by the four Roman Catholic bishops
in Scotland in 1853, and since authorized by Archbishop
Hughes, of New York, says, in answer to the question,
" Must not Catholics believe the Pope himself to be infallible ? "　" This is a Protestant invention. It is no article
of the Catholic faith. No decision of his can bind on pain
of heresy, unless it be received and enforced by the teaching body, that is by the bishops of the Church." And,
so, too, the book entitled the " Faith of Catholics," by
Messrs. Kirke and Berington, a standard authority with
the old Gallican party, though lately manipulated by
Mgr. Capel, so as to bring into harmony with Vaticanism,
asserted before it had undergone this manipulation, Prop.
XIV.: " It is no article of the Catholic faith to believe
that the Pope is in himself infallible, separated from the
Church even in expounding the faith ; by consequence
Papal definitions or decrees, in whatever form pronounced,
taken exclusively of a General Council on acceptance by
the Church, oblige none, under pain of heresy, to interior
assent." A formal contradiction this of the Vatican dogma.

Prop. XV.: " Nor do Catholics believe that the Pope has
any direct or indirect authority over the temporal con-
cerns of states, or the jurisdiction of princes. Hence,
should the Pope pretend to absolve his Majesty's subjects
from their allegiance on account of heresy or schism, such
dispensation they would view as frivolous and null." A
direct contradiction of the XXIII. proposition of the
Syllabus. For thirteen centuries an incomprehensible
silence on this now fundamental article reigned throughout the whole Church and her literature. None of
the ancient confessions of faith, no catechism, none

of the patristic writings composed for the instruction of the people, contain a syllable about the Pope, still less any hint that all certainty of faith and doctrine depends on him. I have said enough to show you that the Roman Church differs widely from the Catholic Church in her organization, government, and mode of diffusing and propagating the truth; and that in the fundamental article of her belief she is in flat contradiction to the voice of the whole Catholic Church, and of her own teaching till quite recently. I had hoped to have time to trace in this lecture the origin and progress of this divergence of the Roman from the Catholic Church, but I must leave it for another lecture. I have used strong language about the foundation upon which this departure rests. I promise to justify that language abundantly. May God defend the right and maintain His own truth amid all the strife and errors of human frailty and passion. May He ever purify and defend His Church, and bring us all by His own mighty power to a knowledge of and agreement in the truth.

NOTE A, LECTURE II.

* As the truth of these statements is recklessly denied in Ryder's reply to Littledale, the following statement of the case by the Rev. J. M. Davenport (Papal Infallibility, pp. 89-90-91), will enable the reader to judge :

"The case of Honorius is so stubborn a fact that Roman apologists have been driven to many strange expedients to get rid of it. (I condense from *Church Quarterly Review*, April 1879, p. 18):

1. Baronius alleged the insertion of Honorius' name to be an interpolation and forgery. Driven from that position by closer enquiry, it was said—

2. Honorius was really orthodox, and was condemned by the Council in error; or that

3. He was condemned only in his capacity as a private doctor, since his letter to Sergius was not put forth *ex cathedrâ* ; or

4. He was condemned, not for heresy, but for apathetic negligence in suppressing the heresy of others.

Père Gràtry has fully exposed the ludicrous nature of these shifts to contradict plain history. *Letters to Dechamps.*

One or two quotations from the Acts of the sixth Council will best reveal what the Church thought which condemned Honorius. The council said, Sess. xiii.: "We, taking into consideration the *dogmatic* Epistles which were written by Sergius, Patriarch of the Imperial City (Constantinople at that time), both to Cyrus, who was the Bishop of Phasis, and also to Honorius, Pope of Old Rome, and likewise the Epistle in reply from him, that is, Honorius, to the aforesaid Sergius, and *finding them to be in all respects alien from Apostolic doctrine*, and from the definitions of the Sacred Synods, and of all the Fathers of repute, but following the false doctrines of the heretics, *we wholly reject them, and pronounce them accursed as hurtful to souls. . . .* With these, we have provided that *Honorius, who was Pope of Old Rome, be cast out of the Holy Catholic Church of God, and be anathematized,* because we have found, by the writings which he addressed to Sergius, *that he followed his opinion in all respects and affirmed his impious tenets.*"

In another place, after much the same preamble, they anathematize Honorius: "Since we find in his letters to Sergius that he follows in all respect his error, and *authorises his impious doctrine.*"

Sess. XVI.—occur the words, "Anathema to Theodore the heretic, anathema to Sergius the heretic, anathema to Cyrus the heretic, *anathema to Honorius the heretic*, anathema to Pyrrhus the heretic."

Sess. XVII.—we read, "But since there has never, from the beginning, ceased to be an inventor of evil, who found the serpent to help him, and thereby brought poisoned death on mankind, and so finding suitable tools for his own purpose,—we mean Theodorus, . . . and also Honorius, who was Pope of Old Rome."

These decrees were signed, without any objection being raised, *by the legates of the Pope Agatho*, and by all the 165 Bishops present.

The anathema of Honorius was expressly repeated in the letter of the Council to the Emperor, and in its other letter to Pope Agatho, *both signed by the Pope's legates.*

Next Leo II., Agatho's successor, wrote to the Emperor on May 7, 683 A.D., a formal letter in which he says, amidst much else: "We likewise anathematize the inventors of the new error; that is, Theodore, . . . Sergius, . . . and also *Honorius,* who did not keep this Apostolic Church pure with the doctrine of Apostolic tradition, but *endeavoured to overthrow the unspotted faith by his profane betrayal.*"

Either Honorius fell into deadly heresy and so was not infallible, or Leo

II., and at least twenty other popes who anathematised him as a heretic were not infallible.

None of these, we see, charge Honorius with mere negligence, but with positive error.

Again, Leo II. renewed this anathema in his letter to the Spanish Bishops, inviting them to accept synodically the decrees of the Council, in which he tells them that "*Honorius is damned to all eternity.*"

Le Page Renouf, a Roman writer, has drawn attention to a fact which quite disposes of the plea that the sixth Council condemned Honorius in ignorance. At the fourth session of the Lateran Council, held only eleven years after the death of Honorius (viz., A.D. 649), under Pope Martin I., in a dogmatic letter from Paul, the Patriarch of Constantinople (who was condemned as a heretic), Paul claimed Sergius and Honorius as teaching the same heresy as himself. Labbé Conc., Tom vi., col. 227. Both Pope and Council heard this read, and not a word of contradiction was offered ; " a sure sign," says Renouf, " that the cause of Honorius was no longer held to be defensible."

Honorius' name appeared in the Breviaries among the heretics till the sixteenth century : his name was then omitted in new editions, and many of the old manuscript copies were mutilated with a knife. That rather looks as though the Ultramontanes of those days thought his condemnation made against Papal Infallibility.— *Church Quarterly Review*, Vol. viii., p. 20.

It may be well here to observe that in the most authoritative modern defence of Honorius, most of the old positions are forsaken. Pennacchi's treatise "De Honorii, etc.," which appeared at Rome in 1870, and was sent to all the Bishops of the Vatican Council, is fortified by two important "*nihil obstats*" and two "*imprimaturs,*" and is moreover recommended by Cardinal Manning to his clergy. Pennacchi, by his admissions, completely cuts away the ground from under the feet of the majority of his co-apologists. He admits the genuineness of all the documents once called in question. He admits that Honorius wrote his letters to Sergius, not as a private person, but as Pope, with all the authority which that position could give him ; that they were constantly appealed to by Monothelites in support of their heresy ; that Honorius was actually condemned and anathematized as a heretic by the sixth Council *in precisely the same sense* as the other Monothelite heretics were condemned. He admits that the distinction between the Pope speaking as Pope *ex cathedrâ* and as a private person is *of modern invention.* He admits that language occurs in the Epistles of Honorius which, *had they been written by a heretic*, nothing in the world could save from being accounted undoubtedly heretical. ("Siquidem si Epistolæ Honorii, a Monothelitis scriptæ sunt, ab hæresi excusari non possunt.") But he avoids the conclusion which would naturally be drawn from this, by taking for granted that Honorius was not a heretic, and that therefore the language of his letters *cannot* be heretical. Fallacies and assumptions, to a very large extent, do duty for arguments and proofs.

He attempts to establish three points :

1. That the letters of Honorius are not, as a fact, heretical, *i.e.*, they are patient of a Catholic interpretation.

2. That the sixth Council exceeded its powers in condemning Honorius, and that therefore the condemnation is null and void.

3. That Leo II. condemned him, not for heresy, but for negligence.

A remarkable specimen of the writer's ability for making language mean just what at the moment he wishes it to mean, occurs on p. 164, where he explains Honorius' assertion—"We confess *one* will in our Lord Jesus Christ to be equivalent to an acknowledgment of *two* wills, *only in different language.*" In the process of saving Honorius, the reputation of the Fathers of the sixth Council and of several Popes, suffer considerably. (See Willis on Honorius, Appendix). There is no reason, if Pennachi's line of argument be sound, why the rest of the heretics condemned with Honorius should not be whitewashed, or why we should accept the sentence of any Council whatever on any heretic in the past, and not re-open every judgment. The new "Catholic Dictionary" (so-called), bearing the imprimatur of Cardinal Manning, treats the case of Honorius much in Pennacchi's fashion. After admitting the facts of his condemnation by Council, Papal Legates, and Popes, the author struggles to prove him orthodox (that the Council in fact did not know what it was about) ; that the Council lacked such Papal authority as would make its decisions binding ; that Honorius was not teaching *ex cathedrâ*, because he abstained from definitely imposing his own belief on the Church.

This article, like Pennacchi's treatise, will doubtless go down with those who are anxious for some way out of the difficulties, but it cannot satisfy thoughtful persons, whether Roman, Greek, or Anglican.

NOTE B, LECTURE II.

*Connolly, Archbishop of Halifax in his speech prepared for the Vatican Council and afterwards published by himself said in speaking against the infallibility dogma. "We Bishops have no right to renounce for ourselves and our successors the hereditary and original rights of the Episcopate—to renounce the promise of Christ I am with you to the end of the world. But now they want to reduce us to nullities, to tear the noblest jewel from our pontifical breast-plate, to deprive us of the highest prerogative of our office, and transform the whole Church and the Bishops with it into a rabble of blind men. Among whom is only one who sees. So that they must shut their eyes and believe whatever he tells them."

LECTURE III.

THE ORIGIN OF THE PAPACY.

Walk about Zion and go round about her ; tell the towers thereof.

Mark ye well her bulwarks, consider her palaces ; that ye may tell it to the generation following.—Psalm xlviii, 12, 13.

IN following out this injunction we have already seen that the Catholic Church as she came forth from the hands of apostles and apostolic men was a visible, organized spiritual kingdom, with constitutional government, all her bishops being invested with equal spiritual authority and jurisdiction, and all her doctrines defined and maintained, not by one man for all, but by the testimony and judgment of all for each individual. We saw, too, that the Church of Rome differs now, fundamentally, from this original constitution and order ; that she has subverted this representative government, has silenced this universal testimony, and has swept away this legislative control of all questions of morals and of discipline. For this she has substituted an absolute autocracy ruled by one irresponsible head, who has plenary and absolute power, not only over the whole Church, but over the

c

whole world. For Gregory the Great (Pope Hildebrand)
maintained (and the Roman Church is committed to his
position) that the Pope is by Divine right the universal
and paramount lord of the world ; that all monarchs held
their dominions as fiefs of the Holy See, and that the
bishops and clergy formed the court of the suzerain Pontiff. In virtue of these assumed powers the Bishops of
Rome claimed the right, and, by taking advantage of the
necessities of kings and princes, were allowed, in many
lands, the right, not only to control the appointments of
bishops and pastors, and to interfere in the affairs of
national Churches, but to depose kings and princes, to
take away their dominions, and to bestow them upon
whomsoever they would.

The question for to-night is, How was this change
brought about ? How did this power grow up ? And
why was it suffered to exist and to exercise such
influence, as it unquestionably did exercise, both in the
Church and in the world ? Manifestly, from what has
been said, it did not spring into being all at once. And
it manifestly did not exist from the beginning. This
is placed beyond dispute by an authority to which our
Roman Catholic brethren must bow. For when that
which was afterwards known as the Papal system was
first broached, in words only, in the year 598, it was repudiated with horror by Gregory I., the best and greatest
of the Popes. When John of Constantinople, who was
eager to be acknowledged as primate of the Christian
world, had assumed in a public document the title of
œcumenical or universal Bishop, Gregory, burning with
indignation, wrote :—" The one sole head of the Universal

Church is Christ, and I confidently affirm that whoever calls himself or desires to be called Universal Bishop is in his pride the forerunner of Antichrist." (Ad. Imp. Maur., vii, 33.) "No one," he says, "of my predecessors ever consented to use so profane a term." (Epp. Lib. v. 43, ad. Eulog.) "Therefore," he says, "presume not either to give or to receive letters with this false title of universal. Far from Christian hearts be that blasphemous name, in which the honour of all priests is taken away, for on this theory the Pope has the plenitude of power, all other bishops are only his servants, from him all power is derived, and he is concurrent ordinary in every diocese, for œcumenical Bishop means sole bishop. If, therefore, the œcumenical Bishop should err the whole Church would fail."* This was the judgment of Pope Gregory on the doctrine of the Papal supremacy in its ecclesiastical aspects merely. It proves beyond dispute that the claim to this supremacy had not been put forth at the very end of the sixth century. And as all Popes, according to the Vatican decree, have been alike infallible, when speaking on questions of doctrine, it therefore follows that all the Popes who since the time of Gregory VII. have claimed this title and headship have, according to the judgment of their infallible predecessor, been forerunners of Antichrist. The Papal system was evidently unknown at the time of even the sixth and last general council, A.D.. 680. It is not referred to or thought of in any of those great councils, or in the

---

*This ex cathedra utterance of Gregory I. is according to the Vatican decree infallible, and contradicts in explicit terms the infallibity decree of that council.

provincial councils held in England, France and Germany. And the same is true of the earlier North Italian and African councils.

And yet there is no doubt that the germs out of which this huge system has been developed are discoverable at an earlier period than this. The claim grew out of the Roman primacy. Our Lord tells us that His kingdom is not of this world ; it does not seek to usurp the powers of earthly kingdoms, or use their methods or pursue their ends ; and so the Church did not set itself to overturn the orders of human society or to subvert human governments. Its object was to leaven them with its own regenerating principles, and thus to purify and elevate, and strengthen and reform them. It therefore conformed itself as far as possible to the usages of the different parts of the empire and of the other nations into which it spread, and for the purposes of its own government adopted their civil divisions. The synods of the different nations, or provinces, or larger divisions of the empire, assembled at the metropolis or capital city of each. The bishop of such a city would naturally be given precedence and elected chairman of the council. Hence there grew up a system of metropolitans. And in process of time the bishops of the capitals of the three great continental divisions of the empire, Antioch, Alexandria and Rome, were by a sort of tacit consent accorded the presidency of the councils which from time to time assembled at one or other of these great centres. Their bishops were early entrusted with the guardianship and enforcement of the canons adopted at these councils, and with a certain supervising power over the other bishops in their respective divisions. After a while they were called Patriarchs, though not till after the time of the first Council of Nice, which recognized the order that had grown up; and as questions of precedency had begun to be agitated, the council fixed the limits of each of these metropolitical sees and confined that of Rome to the city and suburbicarian provinces—that is, to Southern Italy, Corsica, Sardinia, and to Sicily—to which by a decree of the general Council of Nice the legitimate jurisdiction of the Bishop of Rome is still confined.

At the same time a primacy of honour and precedency was accorded to Rome, not because, as is now claimed, it was the See of St. Peter, but simply and solely because Rome was the capital of the empire. This origin of the precedency accorded to Rome among the other patriarchates is distinctly stated on the highest possible authority, viz., that of two general councils, Constantinople and Chalcedon, to have been political and not religious. It was because Rome was the capital of the empire, " the mistress city," and not because it was the see of Peter, that the primacy was given to it. And when Constantinople became the second capital, it was raised by the second general council to the honorary dignity of a patriarchate, and precedency was assigned to it over Alexandria and Antioch, and next after Rome, " for as much as it is New Rome." But this primacy of Rome was entirely titular and honorary. It did not entitle the Bishop of Rome to interfere in any other patriarchate than his own. The Patriarchs of Alexandria and Antioch had each the same authority over their respective provinces as he of Rome had over his. The metropolitan jurisdiction was the same which every metropolitan exercised in his own province.   Milan was another metropolitan see in Italy ; and while Ambrose was archbishop there, it entirely overshadowed Rome.   Aquilia and Ravenna were two other metropolitan sees and centres of ecclesiastical government in Italy. And each was entirely independent of Rome, acknowledging only a primacy of honour in that see.   This primacy of honour, however, soon began to be pressed by the occupants of the Roman see into one of right and jurisdiction.

In very early times the Churches which had been founded by the Apostles themselves were looked up to with considerable and natural respect as a sort of models of apostolic faith and discipline.   It was naturally assumed that the mind and teaching of the Apostles would be better known and remembered in these Churches than elsewhere; and so when difficulties or disputes arose, they were naturally referred by mutual consent to these apostolic Churches for solution ; and as Rome, in addition to being the capital city of the empire, was the only apostolic see in the Western Church, these appeals from the west were naturally made to her.   But as Rome stretched her pretensions she asserted herself to be *the* apostolic see, and claimed to be invested with appellate jurisdiction, and to be a court of final appeal for the whole Church.   Some of the fathers had made reference to this respect for apostolic *sees*, and councils had recognized appeals to them.   Rome endeavoured in later days to fortify her pretensions by the falsification of these evidences, making them speak of the apostolic *see* instead of the apostolic *sees*, as they actually did. (Mansi concil ix., 716 and 732.)

The absence of the Emperors and the court from Rome during the time that Christianity was becoming the religion of the masses—added to the ruin of the empire with its ancient families by Alaric and Attala —left the bishop beyond question the greatest personage in Rome and one of the greatest in Italy. And as his influence, so his pride and ambition grew apace. The imperial city was sinking into insignificance, and some other and more persuasive foundation for the assumed superiority of the Bishop of Rome was sought for. Then the theory that the primacy was based upon the alleged primacy of Peter among the apostles was put forth and made the basis of the claim of the Papacy to univsrsal supremacy. That theory was manifestly an afterthought. It assumes (1) that Christ gave St. Peter the supremacy over the other apostles; (2) that St. Peter's see was at Rome; (3) that the supremacy which Christ gave to St. Peter was to descend to his successors in that see. We reply that there is no evidence in Holy Scripture or primitive antiquity that Peter possessed any such supremacy. It was St. James and not St. Peter who presided at the first great council in Jerusalem, and who formulated and declared the decision, the very office which even liberal Roman Catholics now attribute to Peter's assumed successor. Would any ordinary apostle have presumed to preside and give judgment in the presence of the Prince of the Apostles, the infallible head and universal teacher of the Church ? Would any ordinary bishop ? Would Archbishop Lynch presume to preside, or be allowed to preside, in a general council, while the Pope sat by speaking and voting as an ordinary member ? Would any bishop of the Roman obedience now withstand the Pope to his face, and proclaim to the world that he was to be blamed in his teaching on a point that involved both doctrine and discipline ? As St. Paul tells us, he withstood and denounced St. Peter. Would any Roman Bishop declare now that he was not a whit behind the very chiefest bishops, including the Pope ?

There are three texts which the Roman controversialists adduce to support the assumed supremacy of St. Peter : 1st. " Thou art Peter, and on this rock I will build my church." (Matt. xvi., 18.) The rock, however, does not mean Peter ; and if it did it would not prove that St. Peter was universal bishop and supreme ruler of the Church. But the word translated Peter does not mean a rock at all. For just as there are two words in English, viz., stone, meaning a detached piece of rock, great or small, and rock, meaning a solid mass, so there are two corresponding words in Greek. Now, if the Lord had meant to say that He would build His Church on Peter, He would have said, thou art Peter, O Petros, a stone, and upon this Petros, stone, I will build My Church. But He changed the word to the feminine Petra, thou art Petros, a stone, and then not upon this stone, but upon this Petra, this rock which thou hast just announced, this Christ, this Son of the Living God, will I build My Church.

It has been said in answer to this that our Lord spoke in Syriac, as some say, or in Syro-Chaldaic, as others, and that in that language He did not change the word from stone to rock, but used the same word in both clauses, saying, Thou art Cepha, and upon this Cepha I will build my Church. The reply is that this rests upon mere guess work, for it is not known now whether our Lord spoke at that time in Greek or in Syriac.

2ndly. If this unproved assertion first made by Bellarmine were true, still we should be obliged to accept the variation of the Greek, for the inspiring Spirit caused the truth which our Lord uttered to be recorded in that language for the guidance of all generations. But 3rdly. It so happens (though Bellarmine did not know it) that both the Hebrew and the Syriac word, when it means rock is feminine, but Cephas, denoting a man's name, is masculine, and on turning to the passages in the Syriac version, we find that the feminine pronoun is actually united to the second pronoun, and not to the first.

Again 4thly. No Roman Catholic can use this plea. He is shut out from it because he is bound by the Decrees of Trent to accept the Latin vulgate Bible as his only guide, and that version uses two different words, Petrus and Petram, making the same distinction between a stone and rock that is found in the Greek.

But further, no Roman Catholic teacher, be he bishop, pope or priest, can accept or urge upon others the interpretation upon which the Papal claims are now made, wholly to rest, viz., that the rock means Peter, without involving himself in the guilt of perjury. For the Council of Trent decreed, and "we are bound by a solemn oath," says Professor Dollinger, "which I myself have twice sworn to accept, to explain the Holy Scriptures not otherwise than according to the unanimous consent of the Fathers." Ryder, in his reply to Littledale, seeks to

escape from this difficulty by a very disingenuous
device. In pretending to quote from Littledale he
reverses the requirement of Trent, and makes it read that
no one is to teach anything that contradicts the unanimous consent of the Fathers, and then adds: " Before
unanimity can be contradicted it must be obtained," as
though it were the same thing to say, " Now, you must
not do anything which your Father forbids you to do,"
as to say you must not do anything, except what your
Father tells you to do. The rule of the Council of
Trent is that the clergy must be guided in their
interpretation by the teaching of the Fathers. The rule
of Ryder is that they may teach whatever they like, so
long as it does not contradict the unanimous consent of the
Fathers which he implies cannot be obtained. The learned
Roman Catholic author of Janus asserts that not one of the
Fathers has explained the rock or foundation on which
Christ will build His Church, of the office given to Peter
to be transmitted to his successors, but they understood
by it either Christ Himself, or Peter's confession of faith
in Christ, or often both together, or St. Peter personally to whom the incommunicable privilege of laying the
foundation of the Church by admitting first Jews and
then Gentiles into it was granted. This last interpretation disposes of every one of the patristic witnesses which
Father Ryder quotes against Littledale. The Roman
Catholic Archbishop of St. Louis (Kenrick), in a speech
prepared for the Vatican Council, and published at
Naples in 1879, declares that Roman Catholics cannot
establish the Petrine privilege from Scripture, because of
theclause in the Creed of Pius the IV., binding them to in-

terpret Scripture only *according to the unanimous consent of the Fathers*. And he adds that there are five different patristic interpretations of St. Matt., xvi., 18 : (1) That St. Peter (personally) is the Rock taught by 17 Fathers ; (2) That the whole Apostolic College represented by St. Peter is the Rock taught by eight; (3) That St. Peter's Faith is the Rock taught by forty-four; (4) That Christ is the Rock taught by sixteen ; (5) That the Rock is the whole body of the Faithful. Several who teach the (1) and (2), also teach the (3) and (4), and so the Archbishop sums up thus, " If we are to follow the greater number of the Fathers in this matter then we must hold for certain that the word Peter means not Peter professing the Faith, but the Faith professed by Peter."

And as if to shut the mouths of Roman Catholics, the Council of Trent has decreed that the *Nicene Creed*, " the Symbol of the Faith is the one *firm foundation against* which the gates of Hell shall not prevail." (Sess., iii).

Again in the Roman Breviary the collect for the vigil of St. Peter and St. Paul has the prayer, " Grant, we beseech Thee, Almighty God, that Thou wouldst not suffer us whom Thou hast established *on the Rock of the Apostolic Confession* to be shaken by any disturbances."

But again, even if the Roman interpretation of these passages were accepted as conferring upon St. Peter the same supremacy over the other Apostles as the Pope now claims over all the bishops of the world. Then I ask by what process of reasoning can it be made out that the words " Thou art Peter " confer upon every occupant of the Roman See this assumed supremacy. If in the teeth of the all but universal patristic teaching, the words conferred upon Peter a transmissible office, then how was it transmitted? How is any ecclesiastical office transmitted? Does the place in which an apostle exercised that office, or the chair on which he sat, or the house in which he lived, acting like a charm, confer the office upon every one who may be elected, or who, like Damasus, may elect himself to live in that house, or sit on that chair? Or is it not the case that if Peter had this office it could only be conferred by his own act and ordination.

But if, as Roman Catholics maintain, St. Peter was himself the first bishop of Rome ("fixed his see there") and was martyred while he held that office. Then, clearly, he did not confer his own office by the laying of his own hands upon the second bishop of Rome, who could not be elected till after his death, and if Peter did not confer this supremacy on his successor in the Roman see, who did? Was it one or more of the bishops who were not themselves possessed of it? Could they give to another what they had not themselves? But if to escape this fatal flaw it be maintained without a shred of evidence or authority for it, that St. Peter consecrated his successor before his martyrdom, and conferred his supremacy and infallibility upon him, that will only remove the difficulty one step further on, for that successor did not ordain or consecrate his successor. No Pope does. He is ordained and consecrated and enthroned by other bishops and cardinals who have not the supremacy, and who cannot give it, unless it be contended that the gift resides in the whole Church, which acts through these men, and not in the successors of St. Peter, and that,

of course, subverts the very idea of the Papacy. But if it
be contended that the place, the throne, the see confers this
supremacy, then what have the words "thou art Peter"
to do with it ? The see of Rome is not the Rock, or the
Stone. To make that passage in any way capable of the meaning which Roman Catholics attach to it, it ought to have
been said, " thou art Peter ; upon thy see I will build my
Church, and that see shall confer thine own infallibility
and supremacy upon any man, be he murderer, or adul-
erer, or Simoniac, or thief, who may secure possession of
that throne ?" But even so, how can it be known without
any divine revelation or authority, that the see of Rome,
and not the see of Antioch, where, according to the
explicit statement of Pope Gregory, I., St. Peter re-
sided as bishop for seven years, before he moved to Rome.
How can it be known that the chair of Peter at Rome,
and not that at Antioch, is the one to which this talis-
manic power of charming the man who sits on it into this
supreme ruler and infallible teacher of the Church resides ?

But even this does not end the difficulty. Suppose it
could be proved, or must be believed without any proof or
authority whatever, that the chair of St. Peter at Rome or
his see located there has this power of acting like a charm,
and making men supreme rulers of the church of Christ,
what then becomes of the Avignon Popes who never
touched the chair of St. Peter, never occupied the see ?
Where did they get their infallibility and supremacy; was
it from the French Kings ? or the German Emperor ? Or,
has the chair of St. Peter at Rome the power of acting at
a distance ? And, if so, according to whose will or intention does it act ? The will of secular princes or of the men

themselves who wanted to be Popes ? Or must it be conceded to inexorable logic that the Church during that
whole 70 years, as well as during the Harlot reign, was
as Cardinal Baronius declares without any visible head,
any supreme ruler and infallible teacher. And if for
150 years at one time, and 70 years at another time,
she was without an infallible teacher and guide, what
assurance can we have, on Roman Catholic principles, that
she did not fall into deadly error, and that the very doctrine of infallibility and supremacy, which was greatly
developed during these times, is not itself a delusion and
a snare. It seems to me not an unreasonable inference
that if in the Providence of God the Church was left for
230 years at least without any visible head or infallible
teacher, then no such office was ever intended or constituted in the Church of God, and she has been without it
from the beginning, and is so now.

The text (Luke xxii., 31-32), "When thou art converted,
strengthen thy brethren," does not surely constitute Peter
the one authoritative and only infallible teacher of the
Church; it is merely an exhortation to follow the natural
religious impulse expressed in Psalm li., 12-13. As to
the declaration, "I will give unto thee the keys of the
Kingdom of Heaven," most of the Fathers explain it as
being not the act of gift, but only the promise of that
gift of binding and loosing, which Christ conferred on all
the apostles in common (John xx., 22-23), for they held
the symbol of the keys to mean just the same thing as
the figurative expression of binding and loosing. "Yet,
as Our Lord was pleased to address these words to Peter
only, the better way is to believe that they have a mean-

ing applicable to St. Peter alone. And what that meaning is, is declared by Tertullian, the most ancient, and
indeed for some centuries the only Christian writer who
discusses the question. He says that St. Peter was
granted the incommunicable and unrepeatable privilege
and glory of being the first to unlock the doors of the
Kingdom of Heaven to both Jews (Acts ii., 14-41) and
Gentiles (Acts x., 34-48). And as this was done once for
all, it cannot be done over again by anyone, so that there
is nothing left for the Pope to be special heir to, any
more than the heirs of Columbus, if any be alive, could
enjoy a monopoly of continuing to discover America."
(Littledale.) And indeed, so little satisfied were the
early claimants of papal supremacy with their pretended divine authority for their assumed lordship over
the Church and the world, that they called in the devil
to help them to establish those claims. I am speaking
advisedly and soberly. Cardinal Manning, while he was
still a member of the English Church, said truly, " Men
who use fraud or falsehood or violence or equivocation or
deception to accomplish even righteous ends, do in the
most real and effectual way fall down and worship the
powers of darkness, and make themselves lieges and
worshippers of the devil." Now, it is palpable on every
page of history that when once the Roman pontiffs,
blinded by worldly greed and ambition, conceived the
plan of establishing an absolute ecclesiastical imperialism
over the whole Church, that they presistently resorted to
fraud, and falsehood, and violence of the most inconceivable
wickedness, to overturn the ancient constitution of the
Catholic Church, and to establish their own papal auto-

cracy in its place. Read "Ranke's History of the Popes."
Read "Thierry's History of the Norman Conquest." Read
Fluery's "History of the Church." Read the book entitled "The Papacy," by the Abbe Gattèe. Read Pere
Gratry's "Letters to Dechamp." Read "The History
of the Inquisition," or if you have not time for this,
read the book entitled "The Pope and the Council."
Read Dr. Littledale's "Plain Reasons," and if you do
not stand aghast at the authenticated proof there given
of the deliberate, systematic falsehood and forgery that
were practised, the unscrupulous bartering of every spiritual interest for political power or worldly gain, then it is
because you have no conscience left that can be shocked
by the most unmeasured wickedness.

This work of forgery began before the idea of papal
imperialism was conceived. The very first attempt to
stretch the prerogatives of the primacy into the right
of hearing appeals from other Churches was based
upon a forgery. The great African Church of the
fifth century, with its more than five hundred bishops, had passed a decree forbidding any appeals to be
carried outside its own boundary. Appiarius, a priest of
bad character, had been deposed by an African council.
And he, in spite of the canon, appealed to the Bishop of
Rome, and the Pope, Boniface I. tendered proof through
his legate from the canons of the Council of Nice, giving
the Pope a right to hear appeals from foreign churches.
The bishops assembled at Carthage were amazed; they
had never heard of such a Nicene canon. They had
authenticated copies of the Nicene canons sent from
Alexandria and Antioch, and found that there was no

trace of such a law there, that the pretended canon was a
mutilated copy of a canon passed at the local synod of
Sardica, which was never accepted by the Eastern and
African churches. And so the Synod wrote to the Pope,
rebuking him for the attempted fraud, and telling him
that nothing should make them tolerate such insolent
conduct on the part of the Papal envoys, that is in fact on
his own part, as they were only discharging his commission. (Epist Pontif (Ed Const) p. 113 non sumus
jam istum typhum passuri). This letter was signed,
amongst others, by the illustrious St. Augustin. In
spite of this the same fraud was attempted for the
same purpose by Celestine, 424. And the African
Synod again forced the proof of the fraud upon him,
and emphatically repudiated his claim to jurisdiction.
(Cod. Eccl., Afric., cxxxviii.) The same fraud was attempted by Leo the Great, and for the fourth time
by Felix III., in his attempt to coerce Acacius of Constantinople. (Fleury, Hist. Eccl., xxvii, 43) Again,
the Roman legates at the Council of Chalcedon, 451, produced a forged copy of the Nicene canons, containing in
the sixth canon, the words, "the Roman see has always
had the primacy," of which there is no syllable in the
original, The fraud was exposed in the council to the
confusion of the Roman legates by reading the original.

It is narrated by St. Jerome as a matter of history that
Constantine the Great was baptized on his death bed in
Nicomedia, an Asiatic city, by Eusebius, the bishop.
Nevertheless a fable was invented at Rome in the fifth
century, that the Emperor was a leper and was healed of
his disease by means of baptism administered to him by

D

Pope Sylvester ; and this falsehood, invented for a political purpose which it effectually served, holds its place in the Roman Breviary and is read by every priest on December 31st of each year. Other fabrications followed in the sixth century, e. g., the forged acts of the council of Sinuessa, and the legend of Pope Marcellinus, the forged constitution of Sylvester, the forged gesta of Liberius and Pope Xystus III., the pretended history of Polychrymous, exhibiting the Pope, 435, judging an Eastern patriarch. Then the forged letter of the council of Nice to Pope Sylvester, and his reply, and the acts of the council held by him. Then the famous passage in St. Cyprian's book, on the unity of the Church, was amended by a fabrication which first appears in Pope Pelagius II.'s letter to the Istrian bishops. St. Cyprian said that all the Apostles received from Christ equal power and authority with Peter. This was too glaring a contradiction of the papal claims that were now being put forward, so the Pope interpolated these words, " the primacy was given to Peter to show the unity of the Church and of the chair. How can he believe himself to be in the Church who forsakes the chair of Peter ? " This forgery was quoted as genuine by Archbishop Lynch or by one of his priests, in a controversy with myself a few years ago. Then followed, in the year 730, the first edition of the Liber Pontificalis, every historical notice of which is false. Its special object was to represent the Pope as teacher of doctrine and supreme judge of men. This book thoroughly misled our own Bede and prepared the way in the west for the reception of the fabrications of Isidore. After the middle of the eighth century the fable about the baptism of Constantine by Pope Sylvester is enlarged into the pretended donation of Constantine, a forgery which was successfully palmed off on Pepin, king of France. In 754, Pope Stephen III. forged a letter (still extant, in the name of the Apostle Peter) to Pepin, his adopted son, king of the Franks, in consequence of which that monarch bestowed on the Pontiff a large territory containing more than 20 cities. And this was the foundation and beginning of the temporal power of the Pope. Fleury, in recording this event, describes it as an artifice witout parallel before or since in church history. And another eloquent Roman Catholic writer says it was a falsification which for strangeness and audacity has never been exceeded.

But in spite of these dishonest attempts to push the claims of the Papacy, no change had taken place at the beginning of the ninth century, in the constitution of the Church, as I have described it, and especially none as to the authority for deciding matters of faith. But about the middle of that century, 845, was put forth the fabrication of the Isidorian decretals —a forgery before which all its predecessors sink into insignificance, and which gradually resulted in that complete change of the constitution of the Church which I have described. About a hundred pretended decrees of councils and formal official letters of the earliest Popes were fabricated in the West of Gaul by Isidore Mercator and were eagerly seized upon by Pope Nicholas I., and were used both by him and his successors—especially by Gregory VII.—as genuine documents to support the new and extravagant claims which they put forth.

Dr. Littledale says "that Pope Nicholas I. solemnly and publicly lied about these forgeries, assuring certain Frankish bishops that the Roman Church had long preserved all these documents with honour in her archives, and that every writing of a Pope was binding on the whole Church, knowing as he must have known that not one of these forgeries was or ever had been laid up in their archives." Not only so, but though these forgeries have been known and acknowledged as such for more than three centuries, as, for instance, by Cardinals Baronius and Bellarmine, the two greatest Ultramontane writers, and by Pope Pius VI. himself, who said they ought to be burned; yet they are still wrought into the whole texture of the Roman canon law, which is largely made up of them. They are quoted as genuine in Liguori's "Moral Theology," the chief text book on this subject in the Roman Church, to prove Papal Infallibility, and they have been inserted in a new edition of the Breviary by the above-named Cardinals, who knew that they were false. I think I have said enough to justify my strong language about the forgeries. I can multiply proofs a hundred-fold to any who may desire it, for the system thus audaciously begun was imitated with unfaltering step by many successors, and has been carried on up to our own time. Cardinal Wiseman was deeply involved; and even Cardinal Newman, the soul of truth and honour when with us, has not escaped this terrible contagion and guilt. Forgeries and lies go hand in hand, and are alike the foundation of Rome's practical system to-day. Dr. Littledale, who has searched this subject through and through, says :—" Nevertheless, the Roman Church, which professes to worship him who said, 'I am the truth,' is honeycombed through and through with accumulated falsehood, and things have come to this pass that no statement whatever, however precise and circumstantial, no reference to authorities, however frank and clear, to be found in a Roman controversial book, or to be heard from the lips of living controversialists, can be taken as true, nor accepted, indeed, without rigorous search and verification. The thing may be true, but there is not so much as a presumption in favour of its proving so when tested. Truth, pure and simple, is almost never to be found, and the whole truth in no case whatever. Nor is this to be wondered at when Liguori, the most authoritative teacher of morals in the Roman Church, lays down that equivocation is certainly lawful at all times, and may be confirmed with an oath for a just cause, any cause being just which aims at retaining any good things that are useful to body or spirit, while mental reservation, so long as it is not pure, that is not such unqualified lying as leaves the hearer no possible loophole through which he may, by exceptional shrewdness, guess at the truth, is always lawful for a just cause; and as no cause would be more just in Roman eyes than to win a convert, it follows that every security exists for the use of deceit in controversy." The Rev. E. S. Foulkes, who, in the early days of the Oxford movement, verted to the Church of Rome, but after seventeen years' trial came back to us again in utter horror at what he had proved the Roman practical system to be, writes:—"I have occupied the greater part of my life in the study of ecclesiastical history, first as a member of the Church of England, and then as a member of the Roman communion, and the deliberate conviction to which I was constrained to come, while yet a member of the Roman Catholic body, was this: That if ever there was a system that deserved to have the words 'man-slayer' and 'liar' branded on the most conspicuous part of it, in indelible characters, it is the existing system of the Roman Catholic Church." This charge is more than proved by Pere Grâtry in his letters to Dechamp, which to the utter confusion and dismay of the Papal court were published at Rome during the session of the Vatican Council, page after page teems with instances of the falsification of Fathers, of the decrees of Councils and Popes, of false deduction of garbled passages (chapter and verse given for each), so that he does not hesitate to say, It is a system utterly gangrened by fraud. I have been cramped all through for time. I have, however, said enough to show, not only that the Roman Church differs, in constitution, but that in its inner spirit and life it differs *toto cœlo* from the Catholic Church.

On Sunday evening next I will go with Archbishop Lynch in examining the practical results of the system that rests upon this foundation. May the Holy Spirit of Truth descend in all his illuminating, convicting power upon those who thus come to us demanding our submission with a lie in their right hand. May He lead them back into the land of righteousness and truth, and give them repentance true and deep for the sin that they have sinned, not only against their brethren, but against the God of truth, whom they profess to serve.

LECTURE IV.

THE PRACTICAL RESULTS OF PAPAL AUTOCRACY AND INFALLIBILITY.

Walk about Zion and go round about her ; tell the towers thereof.

Mark ye well her bulwarks, consider her palaces ; that ye may tell it to the generation following.—Psalm xlviii, 12, 13.

IN endeavouring to follow out the duty to which we are here called, we saw last Sunday evening that the Papal system of the present day is not the Catholic Church ; that it is a mere disfiguring excresence on the organization of the Church, hindering and discomposing the action of its vital powers, and bringing manifold evils in its train. Further that it is an excrescence which had no existence at the beginning—which in its faint outline was rejected with abhorrence by Pope Gregory the Great, at the very end of the sixth century, and which only gradually developed itself into its present portentous proportions, and won its way to acceptance in the tenth and following centuries. It based itself first upon the invention of the untenable Petrine claims, and then upon forgeries and falsifications endless, which from the sixth century for-

ward were put forth and used in the interests of the
Papacy, and became its chief instruments in deceiving,
and then enslaving one after another the nations of Western Europe.   No one acquainted with the history of the
times can for a moment doubt that the Papal sovereignty
over the Church and the world, as proclaimed by Hildebrand and his successors, grew out of and rests upon these
forgeries.

   We would naturally suppose that men could not thus
lay unauthorized hands upon the ark of God ; that they
could not thus, according to Cardinal Manning's teaching,
call in the devil to help them to re-fashion the Catholic
Church without the Divine vengeance overtaking them
sooner or later.   Archbishop Lynch, however, tells us
that the reverse of this is the case; that the house whose
walls were thus built up of forgeries and falsehood stands
before us to-day as the very ideal of perfection and sta-
bility, the owned of God, the admired of men, the one
only refuge for sinners. The Scripture, he says, interpreted
by the teaching body of the Catholic Church, that is, by
the Pope and bishops in council, "is unity and doctrine.
No two Catholics can differ from one another ; the same
doctrine is preached in Rome, China, Australia and
America."   And over against this picture is exhibited in
bright light the confusion and contradictions that prevail
amongst those who claim to interpret the Scriptures
according to their own private judgment.   And no doubt
the contrast as painted by the Archbishop is very impres-
sive to many minds.   Thoughtful people feel that the
divisions and strifes among Christians are a shame and a
weakness, and plain people can see from their own Bibles

that this alienation of those who believe in the one Lord
Jesus Christ and worship the one God and Father is not
according to the mind of Christ Jesus ; nay, that it is a
direct contradiction of His will.   And many a distracted
soul has longed for some voice of authority that could
command and quell the strife, some infallible teacher that
could proclaim the truth without the possibility of mistake
or error, and in very weariness of the strife some—not
many—have resolved to stifle their own reason, and conscience and knowledge of the facts of history, and seek to
divest themselves of their own individual responsibility
by submitting unconditionally to him of Rome, who claims
to be divinely appointed and inspired to discharge this
very office among men.

The idea is a fascinating one. It seems to attain by the
shortest road, in the simplest way, and with the least
waste of time, what the ancient Church spent so much
trouble upon, agitated and discussed for so long a time,
and only settled at last by the slow and expensive process
of a council. If infallibility can be accepted as a rule of
faith, it becomes a soft cushion on which the mind, as
well of cleric as of layman, may repose and abandon itself
to undisturbed slumber. It is so much easier to hand the
whole matter over to one individual to settle for us,
than to be always " contending for the faith," always
" examining ourselves whether we be in the faith," always
" taking heed to ourselves and to the doctrine," always
" proving all things that we may hold fast that which is
good."   But the fact that it would be easier for us if the
Roman claims were true, does not prove that they are true.
The ostrich, wearied with the race, thinks that it would

be easier just to hide its head in the sand than to toil on
any longer. The young dreamer thinks that it would be far
easier if someone would leave him a large fortune than
for him to have to earn his bread all his days in the sweat
of his brow.   But God, who knows what is best, has decreed that it is better for him and for the vast majority of
fallen men to have to toil on to the end to secure a subsist-
ence. So, too, it would be easier to be put in possession at
once of all knowledge and all truth. But God has willed that
for the exercise and improvement of our faculties, for the
trial of our faith, for the increase of our spiritual life, we
must attain to the one and the other by study and thought,
and toil and care ; and in the exercise of that study and
toil His Church, in which the Holy Spirit dwells, as the
one only Vicar of Christ upon earth, is our infallible
teacher, lighting us on our way by her testimony through
all her history to those great truths which she has witnessed to and defined in her general councils, and proclaimed in her creeds.

But to return to Archbishop Lynch. He tells us that
the Holy Scriptures are to be interpreted by the teaching
body of the Catholic Church, that is, by " the Pope and
bishops in council."   The definition, you will observe, is
an odd one.   It is not the Roman Catholic definition.
" The bishops and council " are thrown in for Protestant
ears. The Vatican decree is that when the Pope, without
any reference to bishops or council, discharges " the office
of pastor and teacher of all Christians, he is possessed of
infallibility in defining doctrines concerning faith and
morals, and that these definitions are of themselves irreformable, because they are the decrees of the Roman

Pontiff, and not because of the consent of the Church."
That is without reference to either the bishops or council
which Dr. Lynch throws in. The meaning of this is explained by Bellarmine, the great Ultramontane doctor, to
be this : " Whatever doctrine it pleases the Pope to prescribe, the Church must receive ; there can be no question
raised ; she must blindly renounce all judgment of her
own, and firmly believe that all the Pope teaches is absolutely true, all he commands absolutely good, and all he
forbids simply evil and noxious. For the Pope can as
little err in moral as in dogmatic questions. Nay, he goes
so far as to maintain that if the Pope were to err by pre-
scribing sins and forbidding virtues, the Church would
be bound to consider sins good and virtues evil." (De
Rom. Pont. IV., 5, p. 456.) Or, as Bishop Cornelio Musso,
of Bitonto, expresses it : " What the Pope says, we must
receive as though spoken by God Himself. In divine
things we hold him to be God. In matters of faith I had
rather believe one Pope than a thousand Augustines,
Jeromes or Gregories." (Consciones in Ep ad Rom.
p. 606). Or, as a Jesuit Father has it : " When the Pope
speaks on a doctrinal question everyone must sacrifice
his understanding and submit blindly, and especially the
bishops as patterns to their flocks."

This is what Archbishop Lynch parades as the Catholic
mode of interpreting the Scriptures. But I beg to
tell his Grace that it is just as far from the Catholic
mode of interpretation as is that of the man who in
the exercise of his private judgment claims the right to
attach any meaning to the sacred words that may com-
mend itself to him. The Catholic doctrine, as to interpre-

tation, is that neither the individual man nor an individual Pope has any right to "prescribe," as Bellarmine expresses it, any doctrine whatever. The faith was once for all delivered to the saints. No new doctrines can be found out or imposed. The whole Church in her corporate capacity is the divinely appointed interpreter; but even the Church cannot disclose any new doctrine. She cannot create anything, but only protect and witness to, and explore and define, and apply the deposit she has inherited. She does not give opinions or express judgments as to what she thinks the truth is, or ought to be; she bears witness to what the truth from the beginning has been. And the meaning of a judgment passed in one of her councils, on any point of doctrine is simply this: "Thus have our predecessors, back to the days of the Apostles, believed, thus do we believe, and thus will they who come after us believe, for this was the doctrine delivered to the saints from the beginning."

So that the mode of interpretation to which Archbishop Lynch and the whole Roman communion is now committed, though he calls it Catholic, is as radically and totally different from the Catholic mode as that of the extremest Protestant. It is in effect precisely the same thing. The one sets up his individual self, and the other the individual Pope, not as the investigator of and witness to the old truth, but as the inventor and imposer of new truths. But however radically the Roman mode of interpretation may differ from the Catholic, Archbishop Lynch tells us it works admirably well. It has produced "unity of doctrine;" no two Catholics can differ from one another, etc.

But has the Archbishop forgotten the difference that is raging at the present time between the maximizers who so interpret the doctrine of the infallibility as to claim divine authority for every casual utterance of a Pope on any religious or moral question, and of the minimizers who, regardless of the Vatican decree, hold that the Pope is only infallible when he proclaims a decision at which a general council has arrived ?   Cardinal Manning heads the one party in England (Petri privilequim, pp. 34-39) and Cardinal Newman (letter to the Duke of Norfolk) leads the other.   Has his Grace forgotten the absolute contradiction between the teaching of the Irish, Scotch, and American episcopate about the question of the Pope's personal infallibility and his own enforced teaching now ? When he speaks of unity of doctrine, has his Grace forgotten that Cardinal Newman denounces as a "bad dream" that teaching about the Blessed Virgin which is found in Liguori's "Moral Theology ?"   Has he forgotten the fierce doctrinal struggle between the Jesuits and Jansenists, both recognized by Popes as good Catholics till the Jesuits gained the mastery over the Papacy itself ?   Has his Grace forgotten the jealousies of the rival religious orders, as, for instance, that which raged for centuries between the Franciscans and Dominicans, a strife which involved grave questions of theology, and which was carried on with exceeding rancour and bitter hostility.   Does he forget that it was the disputings and quarrellings between the Jesuit, Franciscan, Dominican and Capuchin orders, which wrecked and ruined the hopeful beginnings of their missions in China ?   Does he forget that the various orders which arose in the Latin Church precisely

resembled the Protestant sects and far surpassed them in
denominational rivalry and rancour ? Does he forget the
strife between the regulars and the parochial clergy, between the Jesuits and Seculars ? Does he forget the 39
anti-Popes and the powerful factions which followed
them and deluged the land with blood ? Does he not
know that in a large number of instances the duly elected
Pope was set aside merely because his intruding rival had
stronger friends, larger armies and a longer purse ? Does
he forget that Pope Damasus, elected by the Arian fac-
tion, settled the dispute between himself and Ursinicus,
elected by the Catholic party, by putting himself at the
head of an armed rabble and taking by storm the churches
where his opponents were collected, and that he inaugurated his work of infallible teacher by committing frightful slaughter ? Does he forget that Innocent II., who
was unquestionably the anti-Pope, through the assistance of several European monarchs, ousted Anicletus
II., who had been duly elected, and by the aid of an invading army took his seat on the Papal throne ?

Unity of doctrine, harmony, brotherly love and peace
within the Church of Rome ! It is a beautiful picture, but
where is the reality ? There is actually no Church in the
whole world which has been so openly, so frequently and
so fatally divided and rent by schisms as the Church of
Rome. It is the Church of many and ever-changing religions. It has changed its faith twice within the last
thirty years. There is, no doubt, outward uniformity in
the Church of Rome now, especially when it is under the
inspection of Protestants ; but it is an enforced uniformity, which is obtained by the suppression of reason and
conscience, and historical knowledge and common sense.

And surely if this Catholic interpretation, as Archbishop Lynch calls it, this infallible teaching and guidance be any good, it ought to have produced the unity of which he boasts all along; for the Pope has always been infallible. A costly vase which is offered to our admiration, for its freedom from the smallest flaw must fail to produce the desired effect if the marks of cement and riveting be clearly visible all over it, showing that however skilfully pieced and mended now, it was once shattered to fragments—(Littledale), and is only held in its seeming unity by artificial means. It required the long pontificate of Pius IX., and the gradual filling of almost every see in Latin Christendom with his dutiful nominees to achieve even this result, a result which has been brought about by such a complete divergence from the constitution and teachings of the ancient Catholic Church that Rome is no longer in either respect one with it.[*]

But if it be a divinely revealed dogma, as the Vatican decree asserts, that the Pope is the infallible pastor and

---

[*] And the result of this oppression, as might have been expected, has been to drive not thousands but millions of men out of the Roman Church into the ranks of violent scepticism. And not only so, but the feud between the Liberals and Ultramontanes has become so violent that the Pope himself has been compelled to interfere. The letter of Pope Leo XIII. to the Papal Nuncio at Paris shows how beautiful and inviting the unity of which Archbishop Lynch boasts, really is. Writing to his own special supporters, the Ultramontane journalists, the Pope says, " their passionate controversies, their personal attacks, their constant accusations and recriminations, by adding daily fuel to dissension, render conciliation and brotherly harmony more and more difficult." And then he exhorts them to cease wasting their time and strength in attacking each other and thus giving every advantage to the impious designs of their enemies. This according to the infallible authority, is the truer reality. It corresponds not with the Archbishop's brilliant picture.

teacher of all Christian people when he speaks *ex cathedra*, then one would expect some sort of congruity between the character of the individual and the high office of divinely inspired and infallible teacher which he is called to discharge. One would suppose that the grace which so inspired him, and the sense of responsibility which his high office must carry with it, would at least change and elevate his character; that the grace of infallibility, which is to confer such unspeakable blessings upon the whole Church, would bless him first, who is the subject of this grace. And yet what was the character of the men who occupied the Papal throne in the years that followed the full developement of the Papal claims ? Cobbett, who has been flung at us lately as an impartial historian, whose statements cannot be disproved, says, as a writer in the *Mail* quotes him: "If we look into the history of the Popes we shall find reason to conclude that they were the most abandoned and flagitious of mortals, who hesitated not at the perpetration of any crime to accomplish their purpose. Even popish writers admit that no throne was ever filled with such monsters of immorality as the chair of St. Peter. They are described as having been not only detestable in themselves, but as having given occasion by their example to the perpetration of all sorts of wickedness, imposture, delusion, oppression, robbery, tyranny, murder and massacre." And Cobbett in this instance, had good authority for what he said. For Cardinal Baronius, a most devoted son of the Church, speaking of the Roman Church in the tenth century says : "What was then the semblance of the Holy Roman Church ? As foul as it could be ; when harlots, superior in power as in profligacy, governed at Rome. At whose will sees were transferred, bishops were appointed, and, what is horrible and awful to say, their paramours were iutruded into the see of St. Peter;—false pontiffs who are set down in the catalogues of Roman Pontiffs merely for chronological purposes; for who can venture to say that persons thus basely intruded by such courtezans were legitimate Roman Pontiffs? No mention can be found of their election or subsequent consent on the part of the clergy. All the canons were buried in oblivion, the decrees of the Popes stifled, the ancient traditions put under ban, and the old customs, sacred rites, and former usages in the election of the chief pontiff were quite abolished. * * You can imagine as you please what sort of presbyters and deacons were chosen as cardinals by these monsters." "The Church was then without a Pope, but not without a head. Its spiritual head never abandoned it."

He is describing a period covering the reigns of thirteen Popes, but Gilbert Genebard, Archbishop of Aix, greatly extends the time. He says that during nearly 150 years about fifty Popes had fallen away from the virtues of their predecessors, being apostatical rather than apostolical. (Genebard Chron., sec. IV., Anno 907.). Again, at the end of the fifteenth century, came a group of pontiffs as bad as in the darkest times of the harlot reigns, Sextus IV., Innocent VIII., and worst of all, Alexander VI., the Nero of the Papacy, one of the vilest criminals that ever lived! Though a vowed celibate, he was both the father and the paramour of Lucretia. His election was simonaical, he was chosen Pope by means of pur-

E

chased votes. He systematically sold the cardinalate to the highest bidder, so that there were no true cardinals, because he had no right, by reason of his own simony to nominate at all, and because by their own simony the whole transaction, according to the canon law of the Roman Church, was invalidated. Henry VIII. was a man of pure and noble life when compared with this wretch. Yet this Borgian Pope sat on the altar of St. Peter to be adored as the vicar of Christ, and exercised spiritual jurisdiction over the Church of Christ. These the fruits of the Papal sovereignty ! These the divinely inspired infallible teachers of all Christian people ! When Alexander VI. died there was no validly created cardinal left for the election of a new Pope, so that on Papal principles the Petrine succesion was here irremediably broken, and there has been no valid Pope of Rome since the year 1492. Therefore, according to the strict interpretation of Roman Canon law, there is no apostolic jurisdiction, mission, or succession, left in the world. All the eggs have been put into one basket, and not one has withstood the fall. The English Church, and indeed the whole Catholic Church, can never be reduced to such an absurd position. For the ancient theory expressed by St. Cyprian's well known words " *Episcopatus unus est cujus a singulis in solidum pars tenetur.*" The Episcopate is a unity of which each member exercises to the full all its powers and privileges (literally of which a part is held by each individual for the combined Episcopate, or in joint tenancy). On this old Catholic theory there can never be loss of apostolic jurisdiction or mission, unless every bishop in the world died at the same moment. If only one bishop were left he would possess the power to re-bishop the world. Not so with the Roman Church. All jurisdiction and mission is centered in the Pope. A failure or flaw therefore, in the Papal line brings the whole fabric to the ground." (Rev. Mr. Davenport.)

It will, perhaps, be said that these Popes have never spoken *ex cathedra*. For some Roman theologians of the minimizing school maintain that the Popes up to the present day have only once spoken with the formalities necessary to make their utterances *ex cathedra* and infallibly binding, and that was when Pius IX., on December 8th, 1854, decreed the Immaculate Conception of the Blessed Virgin Mary. But unfortunately that tenet was denounced by orthodox Catholics, including fourteen Popes, for a thousand years, as a heresy, and is contrary to the well-nigh unanimous consent of the Fathers, and therefore, forbidden under oath to be taught by any Roman Catholic divine. And surely if this one pronouncement were the sum total of the benefit which has accrued to the Church by this one-man headship and infallible teacher which Archbishop Lynch tells us is necessary to the Church, it is not worth preaching about, still less is it worth all the forgeries, and blood, and tears which its establishment has cost.

But taking the common sense view of the meaning of the Vatican decree, the one which it was manifestly intended to bear, and grammatically does bear, " that when a Pope speaks publicly on a point of doctrine or discipline, either of his own accord or in answer to questions addressed to him, he does speak *ex cathedra.*" Then where is the great benefit and blessing that has accrued from this subversion of ancient Catholic usage in declaring the truth ? What practical advantage has ever accrued to the Church from the utterances of this infallible teacher ? Not one solitary example is to be found in the whole of Church history of any great struggle or difficult question being decided by the Pope's interference. Not one of the great heresies was put down in this way, but always by a council or by some private theologian. And what reliance can be placed by any sane man on the guidance of infallible teachers, who not only contradict one another, as the Popes flatly and flagrantly do, but more than once contradict themselves ? What help has ever been derived from this infallible voice ? Surely, if ever there was an occasion when that guidance ought to have been used, and to have been of use, it was in the early part of the sixteenth century. "Europe was then," Dr. Dollinger says, "in a state of the extremest excitement, and the whole religious edifice seemed tottering to its fall. The most discordant doctrines in sharp antagonism to all previous teaching were forcing their way to the front. Never had there been a period in all Christian history when the perplexity of men's minds had been so great, and the people left to themselves so utterly helpless, as in the forty-three years from 1520 to 1563." Yet the Popes, according to the latest theory the sole infallible teachers of mankind, kept silence. Not a single doctrinal bull of that whole period exists. One whole generation was suffered to grow up in Europe and another to pass to its grave without knowing what the infallible chair in Rome bade them believe, on the gravest religious questions. German bishops, like Fabre, of Vienna, made the most moving representations. "The whole generation," he said, " whose birth and youth coincided with the time of this great controversy, knew not what was the true religion, and if this continued men would become thoroughly godless and atheistical." But all was in vain; the Popes persisted in their policy of silence. And many who waited and wished for some voice to guide them were swept away in that swelling tide which swept three-fourths of Western Europe out of the Roman obedience.

And this is only an example of what has been and will continue to be the action of this infallible teacher and guide, in every great crisis of human thought, in every great perplexity and trial of faith. What one doctrinal direction of any practical importance, what interpretation, that is of the least help to the Christian in his daily temtations and struggles, has issued from this infallible chair, even since the promulgation of its lofty claims ?—the anti-Catholic creed of Pope Pius IV., the anti-Catholic doctrine of the Immaculate Conception, the atrocious sentiments of the Syllabus, and the self-contradicting doctrine of Papal infallibility. But what help or guidance do they give, even if they were true, to the Roman Catholic in living a Christian life, which is not possessed by other men; and what help can be obtained from this source? The Pope is necessarily so occupied with the mere business of his vast administration that he has no time to devote to interpretations or to teaching, and does not attempt it. But on this head I have said enough.

I should like to have had time to trace the effects of this overthrow of the ancient Catholic constitution and spirit in the practical affairs of the Church and the world.

But I must pass this by and hasten on to the points of doctrinal difference between the Roman Church and the Catholic Church. The Roman Church differs widely from the Catholic Church in constitution, in spirit, in practice, and has reaped as the result of her interference with the House that God built, not strength but strife, and corruption, and weakness, and confusion.

May God the Three in One deliver us evermore from all false doctrine, heresy and schism. May he keep us steadfast in the faith and communion of the Catholic Church.

LECTURE V.

THE WAY IN WHICH THE PAPAL SOVEREIGNTY WAS OB-TRUDED UPON THE CHURCHES OF WESTERN EUROPE.

Walk about Zion, and go round about her : tell the towers thereof.

Mark ye well her bulwarks, consider her palaces ; that ye may tell it to the generation following.—Psalm xlviii., 12, 13.

IN trying to follow out the duty here enjoined we have seen :

1. That the Catholic Church of the first days was a visible, organized society, which began at Jerusalem and extended itself in ever-widening circles, first into one land and then into another, till it filled all the world, and has reached down to us.

2. That for two hundred years we hear nothing of the superiority of one bishop over another.

3. Then, out of the mere necessities of government, as difficulties and disputes arose, they were referred by a natural instinct to churches where one or other of the Apostles had lived and taught, and where it was felt that the apostolic interpretation and traditional usage would be best known.

4. Out of this there grew up the system of metro-political sees, whose bishops presided at the Provincial Synods that were held in their see cities. No doubt, the rank and importance of the city politically, or as a centre of civilization, intelligence and Christian activity, had its weight in determining these metropolitical sees.

5. Then, by an equally natural instinct, the bishops of the capitals of the three great continental divisions of the Empire, Rome, Alexandria, and Antioch, acquired a somewhat similar patriarchal jurisdiction over the metro-politans of the European, African and Asiatic sub-divisions of the one Church.

6. And among these the Bishop of Rome, the capital of the world, was conceded a primacy of honour and pre-cedence. Two general councils solemnly assert that that precedence was based upon Rome's political importance, as the capital of the Empire; and they give no hint of any inherent right she had to that position by virtue of any Petrine claims.

7. The appeals that were naturally made by mutual consent from all parts of the West to the Bishop and Church of the Imperial City—which was also reputed to be the only apostolic see of the West—were soon trans-formed into the rights of an appellate jurisdiction over those churches.

8. This claim was based wholly for a long time on a canon of the local Council of Sardica, which gave the bishops of the provinces represented permission to appeal, not to the bishops of Rome generally, but to a particular bishop of that city, Julius II. The canons of this local synod were, either by accident or design, bound up with

the canons of the General Council of Nice; and the one referring to appeals to Pope Julius was again and again quoted, with necessary changes and interpolations, as a canon of the General Council of Nice, and as binding, therefore, upon the whole Church. This was the only ground upon which the Roman bishops for generations based their claim, not to infallibility, nor even to supremacy, but to the right to hear appeals from other Churches.

9. Then the assumed supremacy of St. Peter over the other Apostles was seized upon, and it was asserted that that supremacy descended from St. Peter to the bishops of Rome, though it is only a vague guess that St. Peter was ever at Rome at all, and a vaguer one still that he was ever bishop of that city; while it is a wholly groundless assumption, without one particle of evidence of any kind to support it, that, even if St. Peter possessed the supremacy ascribed to him, he intended to transmit, or did transmit, that supremacy to the bishops of Rome, and not to the bishops of Antioch or some of the other Churches over which he presided for a longer or shorter period.

10. But as this claim was felt to be too vague and unreliable to support the ambitious projects which the bishops of Rome began to entertain, first of extending their patriarchal jurisdiction, and then of establishing their sovereignty over the whole Church, interpolations and forgeries of the most subversive and wholesale character were resorted to now, to meet every emergency.

I had intended, as I announced last Sunday, to pass from a hurried consideration of some of the effects of this evil work to a brief review of some of the points in which the Roman Church differs from the Catholic Church in doctrine. But, in thinking the matter over, I have felt that in order to present to you a connected view of the progress of events, I ought to point out as well as I can, in the brief space allowed me in this lecture, the way in which the Papal claims that grew out of these earliest forgeries were obtruded upon one after another of the nations of Europe, and won their way to general acceptance.

Nicholas I. was Pope when the forged decretals of Isidore first came to general knowledge. He surpassed all his predecessors in the audacity of his designs. He was greatly favoured by the confusion and ignorance which prevailed during the seventy years of anarchy which followed the break-up of the empire of Charlemagne. Nicholas grasped at the new weapon with eagerness, and silenced the doubts expressed by the Frankish bishops with the assurance that all these forged documents had long been preserved with honour in the Roman archives; and as the object of these forgeries was to represent the Roman bishop as ruler and judge, and teacher of all Churches, Nicholas set himself to inculcate and enforce the principles which they laid down.

For two hundred years after his time, however, the Roman see was not in a position to enforce these claims. They were allowed, therefore, to germinate and spread. They became embedded in the laws and theology and popular belief of the nascent nations.

In the meantime, the Papacy became the prey and plaything of rival factions of nobles, and for a long time of ambitious and profligate women. The Tuscan Counts made it hereditary in their family; again and again dissolute boys like John XII. and Benedict IX. occupied and disgraced the Papal throne, which was now bought and sold like a piece of merchandise, so that nearly three centuries passed before the seed sown by these fabrications produced its full harvest.

Leo IX., who died 1054, inaugurated a new era in the Papacy. The design was now deliberately formed to weld the States of Europe into a theocratic priest kingdom with the Pope at its head. It was Gregory VII., however, who was the first, and in fact the only one of the Popes that set himself with clear and deliberate purpose to subvert the old constitution of the Church, and to introduce a new one. He regarded himself not merely as a reformer of the Church, but as the divinely-commissioned founder of a wholly new order of things. Only Popes and their legates were hereafter to hold those synods by which the Church, for over a thousand years, had regulated her affairs. In every other form the institution was to disappear. He was aided greatly by Anselm, the canonist of Lucca, who first extracted and put into convenient working shape everything in the Isidorian forgeries, for the accomplishment of Papal absolutism ; and next, by altering the law of the Church by a tissue of fresh inventions and interpolations in accordance with the requirements of his party and the standpoint of Gregory.

Gregory himself, in his letter to Archbishop Hermann, of Metz—designed to prove how well grounded is the Pope's dominion over emperors and kings, and his right to depose them—set an example of the sort of work he wanted done, by so distorting and interpolating a letter of Pope Gelasius to the Emperor Anastasius, as to make Gelasius say the very opposite of what he did say, viz : " That kings are absolutely and universally subject to the Pope ; " whereas, what he did say was, "That the rulers of the Church are always subject to the laws of the emperors, only disclaiming the interference of the secular power in questions of faith and sacraments." (Regist. ed. Jaffe, p. 457.)

Anselm and his confederate canonists Deusdedit and Gregory, of Pavia, compiled new text books in which they boldly placed the pretended decrees of Popes that had been forged by Isidore in place of the canons of councils, and thus supplied a pretext for Gregory and his successors in their contest with the princes and bishops of their own day. One main pillar of Gregory's system was borrowed from the false decretals. Isidore in his forgeries had made Pope Julius, about 338, A.D., write to the Eastern bishops, " The Church of Rome by a singular privilege has the right of opening the gates of heaven to whom she will." (Decret. pseud. Is., p. 464.) On this forgery Gregory built his scheme of dominion. How, he asked, should not he be able to judge on earth, on whose will hung the salvation or damnation of men ? (Monum. Greg., ed. Jaffe, p. 445.) And so when Gregory, who was notoriously the first Pope to undertake the dethroning of kings, wanted to depose the German Emperor, he wrote, " To me is given power to bind and to loose on earth and in heaven," Were subjects to be absolved from their allegiance—which he was also the first to attempt—he did it by virtue of his power to loose. If he wanted to dispose of other people's property, he declared, as in his Roman Synod, 1080, "We desire to show the world that we can give or take away at our will kingdoms, duchies, earldoms; in a word, the possessions of all men, for we can bind and loose." (Mensi. xx., p. 536.) Personal sanctity had for some time been ascribed to every Pope. Gregory VII. made this holiness of all Popes, which he said he had personal experience of, the foundation of his claim to universal dominion. (Ep. viii., 21 Jaffe, p. 463.) Every sovereign, he said, however, good before, becomes corrupted by the use of power; whereas, every rightly appointed Pope becomes a saint. We saw last Sunday evening what sort of saints many of them became. But then, to meet this objection, we are told that if they have no sanctity of their own they become saints through the imputed merits of St. Peter. Referring to a document which had been unquestionably forged in the 11th century, Gregory VII. affirmed, in 1081, that according to the documents preserved in the archives of St. Peter's church, Charles the Great had made the whole of Gaul tributary to the Roman Church, and had given to her all Saxony.

"The most potent instrument, however, in extending the new Papal system, was the decretum of Gratian, which, about the middle of the twelfth century, was issued from Bologna, the first school of law in Europe, the juristic teacher of the whole of western christendom. In this work the Isidorian forgeries were combined with those of the Gregorian writers, and with Gratian's own additions. His work displaced all the older collections of canon law and became the manual and repertory, not for canonists only but for the scholastic theologians, who for the most part derived all their knowledge of the Fathers and canons from it. No book has ever come near it in its influence in the Church, although there is scarcely another so crammed full of gross errors, both intentional and unintentional. All the fabrications—the rich harvest of three centuries— Gratian inserted in good faith into his collection; but he also added, knowingly and deliberately, a number of fresh corruptions, all in the spirit and interest of the Papal system." (Janus).

Gratian interpolated without scruple, in order to forward the grand national scheme of making the whole Christian world in a certain sense the domain of the Italian clergy through the Papacy. By falsifying a canon, he makes Gregory the Great order that the Church should protect homicides and murderers (Cans. 72, 134). And he takes great pains to inculcate in a long series of canons that it is lawful—nay, a duty—to constrain men to goodness, and therefore to faith, by all means of physical compulsion, and particularly to torture and execute heretics, and to confiscate their property. This notion took full possession of the mind of Innocent III. (1198-1218), the most powerful of the Popes, who worked out to completion the theories of Papal monarchy which others had propounded. He maintained that the Pope is God's *locum tenens* on earth, set to watch over the social, political and religious condition of mankind, like a Divine Providence, as chief overseer and lord, who must put down all opposition. He wished to make Deuteronomy a code of laws for Christians, that he might get

Bible authority for his doctrine of Papal power over life and death; and so he said that as Deuteronomy meant the second book of the law, it must bind the Christian Church which was the second Church. Yet to accomplish his purpose the words had to be altered. It is there said (Deut. xvii., 12) that if any man will not hearken unto the priest (the vulgate has, I believe, High Priest) and to the judge, even that man shall die. Innocent, by a slight interpolation, made this into a statement that whoever does not submit to the decision of the High Priest (whose place the Pope occupies under the new covenant), is to be sentenced by the judge to execution (Decr. per venerabilem, 4-17).

Leo X. quoted the passage with the same corruption to prove that whoever disobeyed the Pope must be put to death. This same Innocent III. wrote to the Patriarch of Constantinople, that Christ has committed the whole world to the government of the Popes, and he gives as a conclusive evidence of this that Peter once walked on the sea— the sea signifying the nations—whence it is clear that his successors are entitled to rule the nations (Innoc. III., lib. ii., 209). This Pope taught that the Papal power is to the royal and imperial as the sun to the moon, which last has only a borrowed light; or, as the soul to the body, which last exists not for itself but only to be the slave of the soul; and the two swords are a symbol of the ecclesiastical and secular powers, which both belong to the Pope, but he wields one himself and entrusts the other to princes to use at his behest and in the service of the Church. Gregory IX. went still further in the assertion of absolute domination over the State, and maintained that the Pope is lord of the whole world, things as well as persons.

But what sort of world, you ask, was it on which such barefaced fabrications could be palmed off, and in which such monstrous claims could be promulgated and accepted and acted on ? And the answer is that it was a wild world, a world of excessive ignorance and darkness and confusion and strife. We can, I apprehend, form but a faint idea of the utter chaos that followed the break-up of the Western empire, when the old civilization was swept away and the old Christianity trampled down under the feet of the invading heathen hordes. The same state of things followed the break-up of the empire of Clovis, Charlemagne and Charles the Fat. A long period of the wildest chaos succeeded each. There was really no stable, settled order of things in the Western empire till the eleventh century; and the ignorance that prevailed during those centuries, in which the half-civilized and not half-instructed hordes were being gathered by whole tribes and nations into the Christian Church, made it an easy matter to palm off any fabrications that might be offered them. They had no means of protecting themselves ; they could know nothing about the matter except what they were told by their teachers. It was an ignorant and uncritical age, and so thoroughly had these forgeries penetrated the literature and belief of those times that not only kings and princes and ecclesiastics were misled, but the very foremost theologian of these centuries, Thomas Aquinas, was wholly deceived. He accepted in good faith not only the Isidorian, but all the forgeries of the canonists and Popes that were put forth in support of the Papal monarchy, and made them the basis of his practical teaching.

But in addition to the ignorance and credulity of the

age, there were many causes which contributed to the success of these Papal designs. The Popes themselves were
consumed with such overweening ambition and such a
devouring greed for worldly wealth and power, that they
were ever ready to take advantage of the crimes and mis-
fortunes of princes, to strike the basest bargains with them,
and to sacrifice every spiritual interest if they might
thereby promote their own wealth and power. Pepin was
encouraged by the Pope in his contemplated rebellion, on
the understanding that he would revive the forged donation of Constantine and found the States of the Church.
Charlemagne was crowned Emperor of the West, on the
understanding that he would renew and extend the gift
of Pepin. A similar bargain was struck with Louis the
Pious, 817, and with the Countess Matilda, 1079. Gregory
VII. supported the pretender Rudolph, 1081, only after
he had extorted an oath from him to support the claims of
the Church. When King Arnulf, to whom the Bishops of
Germany had bound themselves, desired to obtain the
Imperial Crown, he was given to understand that he could
only secure the support of the Pope, which was necessary
to his success, by compelling the bishops and clergy to
submit to what they now regarded as the intolerable, but,
as they inferred from the decretals, the divinely-imposed
yoke of Rome. William the Conqueror obtained the sanction and blessing of the Pope for himself and his ruthless
array of vagabonds and outlaws in their contemplated
invasion of robbery and spoliation on the distinct agreement that he would punish the Saxons for their resistance
to papal claims, and force the English Church into subjection to the Papal throne.

F

You know how concessions were wrung from Henry
II., John, and Henry IV. And these are only a few instances of the way in which this Papal greed of empire
was pursued and pressed, by taking advange of every
political exigency. The Crusaders and the Military Temp-
lars, who regarded themselves as the legions of the Supreme Pontiff, contributed greatly to the growth of this
power. But the most potent instruments for the extension of the Papal claims were the new religious orders of
Mendicants, which sprung up at the end of the twelfth
century, and which swarmed over the whole Christian
world—Franciscans, Dominicans, Augustinians and Car-
melites, and were the strongest pillars and support of this
monarchy. They were the third great lever whereby the
Old Church constitution and system were undermined and
destroyed. They were completely under the control of the
Popes. They acted everywhere as the agents and instruments of the Papacy. They were wholly independent of
the bishops; they were invested with plenary power to
encroach on the rights of parish priests; they were empowered to set up their own churches wherever they
pleased; and so they laboured for the honour and great-
ness of their Order, and for the Papal authority on which
their prerogatives rested. That authority was literally
doubled through their instrumentality. They became
masters of literature, of the pulpit, and of the university
chairs; they travelled about as Papal tax-gatherers and
preachers of indulgences, with plenary power to inflict
excommunication on whomsoever they would. And thus
the campaign organized at Rome was carried into every
village and every parish in western Europe.

The parish clergy generally succumbed to the mendicants, though there were long and bitter contests. The
bishops, too, though they were at first all but unanimously
opposed to the new Papal autocracy—for they saw that
its success would rob them of their independence and
make them mere puppets in the hand of the Supreme
Pontiff—felt now, their own impotence against this
new power of these monks, strengthened by the terrors of
the Inquisition; and they had, however indignantly, to
bend under the yoke that was now laid on their necks.

In order, however, more completely to subvert the ancient constitution of the Church and the regular administration of dioceses by bishops, Papal legates were from
Hildebrand's time appointed. Sometimes they received
a general commission to visit churches; sometimes they
were appointed for a special emergency; but they were
always invested with unlimited powers, and were expected
to bring back considerable sums of money over the Alps.
They traversed different countries surrounded by a troop
of greedy Italians; and, armed against opposition by ban
and interdict, they held forced synods, the decrees of
which they dictated themselves. With this irregular
jurisdiction of legates there grew up a system of Papal
dispensation and exemption from episcopal control; but
every exempted corporation or monastery had to pay a
yearly tribute to the See of Rome, whose interest it was
to thwart and restrain episcopal authority whenever it
tried to act. And so the bishops, in constant danger of
incurring suspension or excommunication, or of being
cited to Rome for violating some Papal privilege, gave
up all idea of any earnest administration of their dioceses.

And as bishops and corporations were in mutual hostility, so the parochial clergy found opponents and dangerous rivals in the richly-privileged mendicant orders, who were unceasing in their attempts to appropriate the more remunerative functions of the priesthood, and to decoy the people from the parish churches into their own. And thus anarchy in dioceses and wild demoralization of the clergy reached a point one cannot read of in contemporary writers without horror. When appeals came to Rome, as they unceasingly did, on disputed presentations to benefices, or episcopal elections, the question was generally decided in favour of the claimant who had the longest purse, though the Popes often took occasion to oust both the claimants and to appoint a third person who had outbidden them both. Abbot Conrad, of Leichtenav, says : " There is no bishopric or spiritual dignity or parish that is not made the subject of a process at Rome ; and woe to him who comes empty-handed ! Rejoice, mother Rome, at the crimes of thy sons, for they are thy gain. To thee flows all the gold and silver. Thou art become mistress of the world through the badness, not the piety, of mankind." (Chron. p. 321.)

Most elections, as the result of the new Papal enactments, came to be disputed ; and thus a vast number of bishops and others were drawn to Rome and detained there for years by processes spun out interminably, until they either died off in that unhealthy city or carried home with them nothing but debts, disease, and a vivid impression of the dominant corruption. And then the Popes claimed the right to give away all benefices vacated either by death or resignation at Rome.

They began their interference in foreign churches by letters of commendation begging appointments from kings or bishops for their own favourites, but without specifying any particular benefice. So it was still in the 12th century. But before long these recommendations took the form of mandates, commanding the appointment of Italians, nephews, favourites, whom they wished for one reason or another to provide for, enrich or indemnify in foreign countries. Cardinal Nicholas Tudeschi says that "church dignities were so loaded with excessive imposts and extortions that they were always subject to debts, and nothing of their revenues was available for religious purposes." Cardinal Zabarella says: "So completely has the Pope destroyed all rights of all lesser churches, that their bishops are as good as non-existent." And Chancellor Gerson says: "In consequence of the greed and lust of power of the Popes, the authority of bishops and inferior church officers is completely done away with, so that they look like mere pictures in the Church, and are almost superfluous." The theory which was finally maintained by the Popes was that by virtue of the sovereign power and absolute authority belonging to the Vicar of Christ, all benefices of every sort appertained to the chair of St. Peter.

It is needless to say that this pontifical view was never accepted in England either by clergy or laity. There had always been abundant, spirited protests against it, such as those of Archbishop Rich, Bishop Grosseteste, etc. There had been special Acts of Convocation and of Parliament passed to prohibit it, such as the Constitution of Clarendon, the three Statutes of Provisors, etc. Nevertheless,

the Popes continued to sell English benefices and sees,
to draw a large part of their revenue from this abuse.
The mischief which was thus produced is graphically set
out in Gascoigne's Theological Dictionary, published about
1450. Gascoigne was a most devoted son of the Church,
and accepted without a suspicion of its being a mistake
the prevalent belief of his time, in the Divine origin of
the firmly-established Papal sovereignty. He complains
bitterly that the Popes used to sell English benefices and
English sees, and to draw a large part of their revenue
from this abuse. " I know it," he writes, "to be a thing
commonly practised in England, that great and wealthy
persons, never elected to any dignity in the Church, obtain from the King permission to accept a Papal provision
of some dignity, and so by means of large sums of money
sent to Rome, and by the Pope's provisions, become
bishops. In the same way others get to be deans of
Cathedrals. Rome has been the principal wild boar to lay
waste the vineyard of the Church, by reserving to itself
the election of bishops, so as not to give the appointment
to any save they first pay the annates, that is the first,
sometimes the first three, years' income of their sees to
the Pope. She has also destroyed the vineyards of the
Church of God by invalidating the election of all bishops
in England, and by promoting evil persons by agreement
with the King, and by decreeing that all elections of
bishops pertain to the apostolic chamber—that is, the
Pope and the Cardinals—and by calling none a Bishop
unless he be chosen by the Cardinals, and first pay a
thousand marks in gifts to Roman courtiers." "Everywhere," he says, " sons of Belial are appointed to churches

and great offices," being intruded by threats, by gifts, or by carnal favouritism. The foulest crimes are perpetrated and winked at." There is hardly a gleam of light in the picture which this contemporary and friendly historian draws of the condition of the Church. All is confusion, greed, indolence, selfishness, and licentiousness.

Thus, by the use of abundant forgeries, which were made the basis of all law and teaching, and were wrought into the popular mind and belief of the Western Church, by taking advantage of every political exigency to bribe or browbeat kings and princes, by the sentiments created by Crusaders and Knights Templar, by the instrumentality of the mendicant orders and Papal legates, and last, but not least, by the unmeasured employment from the middle of the eleventh century of that most inhuman, most fiendish invention, the Inquisition; thus was the ancient constitution and order of the Church overthrown. Thus was Papal Imperialism established. Thus was it obtruded upon one after another of the nations of the Western Empire.

In the great churches of the Eastern Empire it never gained any foothold or recognition, except that it was accepted for a few months near the end of the thirteenth century, when the Greek Church, deceived by a forgery only second to that of the false decretals, of a spurious catena of Greek councils and fathers supporting the claim of the Pope to be the infallible teacher of the whole world and the absolute monarch of the Church. But the Armenian Church, the most ancient of the national churches founded beyond the limits of the Empire, the great Syro-Persian Church of the early and middle ages, the Ethiopian and Abyssinian Churches, the Greek Church down to our own day, the African for five centuries, and, in the west, the Scoto-Irish and ancient British Churches, remained for centuries autonomous and under no sort of subjection to Rome.

Do we wonder that a usurpation which had thus established itself by falsehood, injustice and cruelty unparalleled in the annals of men, should have been felt even by the men whom it deceived and enslaved to be an intolerable bondage, and that, in the language of the author of Janus, "for four centuries from all nations and in all tongues were thousandfold accusations raised against the ambition, tyranny and greed of the Popes, their profanation of holy things, and their making all the nations of Christendom the prey of their rapacity." And what is still more surprising, that in all this long period no one attempted to refute these charges, or to represent them as calumnies or even as exaggerations. Do we wonder that, in the judgment of Dr. Dollinger, the greatest ecclesiastical historian of this age, a reformation of these monstrous abuses could not have been much longer delayed? Do we doubt that God did avenge His own elect in whom His Spirit dwells : First, by withdrawing His Spirit almost visibly from those who arrogantly claimed to be the only instruments of His inspiring light, and by allowing a long succession of men of such criminal and monstrous character to obtrude themselves into the infallible chair that none who were not wilfully blind could fail to see that these were not, and could not be, the divinely appointed channel for making known the divine will and interpretng the divine councils. And then, secondly, by allowing such bewildering anarchy, such wild demoralization, to follow the triumph and completed establishment of that Papal autocracy which claimed divine authority, that the most ignorant and enslaved of men could not fail to see that this usurping power was the enemy alike of God and of men ?"

LECTURE VI.

THE INQUISITION.

O my soul, come not thou into their secret, unto their assembly;
mine honour, be not thou united.—Gen. xlix. 6.

I HAD intended to pass this truly horrible subject over
with the mere reference contained in my last lecture.
But further consideration of the important part it played
in riveting the chains of the Papacy upon western Europe,
convinces me that it cannot be left out of a consideration
of the means by which the ancient Order and independence of the national and provincial Churches were overthrown, and this terrible autocracy over kings and people
established.

The Inquisition, usually spoken of in the language of
the times as " The Holy Inquisition," or " The Holy
Office," was a separate ecclesiastical tribunal, which was
set up by the Pope at the suggestion of St. Dominic, the
founder of the Dominican Friars for the detection, apprehension, trial and punishment of heretics. It was first
formally established in the year 1209, at the Council of
Avignon, though it had been in practical operation for

twenty years before this date. Pope Innocent III. decreed on his own authority that every heretic should be seized instantly and summarily delivered to the Secular Court to be punished according to law ; all his property to be forfeited ; one-third to be given to the informer, one-third to the court that judged him, and one-third to public works ; his house to be demolished, and his friends fined in one-fourth of their property for the benefit of the State. The accused had no right of appeal. No judge, advocate, or notary was allowed to give them any aid under peril of the loss of his office ; and the clergy were forbidden to minister to them. This was the first rough draft of the Inquisitorial Court. It was afterwards greatly modified in the interests of the Papacy. It was not finally abolished in Rome till the year 1849.

For five hundred years it filled Western Europe with torture, and terror, and groans, and tears, and blood. No one whose information has been derived from the ordinary channels of history, and who has not made this subject a special study, can have any idea of the terrors, the injustice, the cruelty and fiendish barbarity of the Inquisition.

The Emperors, from the time of Constantine, had taken upon themselves to enforce upon their subjects the faith which they themselves professed. But the orthodox rulers had distinguished between heresies, and had only inflicted severe penalties on those whose principles led to moral enormities. But that distinction was given up after the death of Pope Lucius III. 1184, and the view of the ancient church on the treatment of the heterodox was completely changed. She had, it is true, often criminally

encouraged the proceedings of the secular arm in enforcing
her faith upon those who rejected it. She had acquiesced
in the infliction of unjustifiable cruelties upon those whom
the kings undertook to punish for immoral principles or
practices. But she had not constituted herself a court for
their detection and apprehension. She had not taken
upon herself to adjudge them to intolerable tortures and
death. She had not abolished the ancient distinction between mere errors of judgment and deliberate
heresies*. But now all was changed. The ruling
principle of the Papacy from this time forth was that
those are heretics who believe otherwise than the Roman
Church believes, and also those who doubt or dispute the
supreme power of the Pope, in temporal as well as spiritual matters. Every departure therefore from the teaching of the Roman Church, and every important opposition
to any ecclesiastical ordinance, must be punished with
death, and the most cruel of deaths—by fire. Complete
apostacy from the Christian faith, or a mere difference of
opinion on some minor points of order, were all the same;
either, according to the new definitions, was heresy, and
was to be punished with death. Innocent III. (Concil. ed·
Labbe xi. 152) declared the mere refusal to swear, and the
opinion that oaths were unlawful, a heresy worthy of
death, and he directed that whoever differed in any respect from the common way of life of the multitude of
Roman Catholics, should be treated as a heretic.

---

* "In the ancient Church when a bishop had become implicated in the
capital punishment of a heretic only as accuser, he was separated from the
communion of his brethren as Idacius and Ithacius were by St. Martin and
St. Ambrose in 385."

The Inquisition was introduced to enforce these principles—to make the Papal system so irresisitble as to impede any disclosures of the rottenness of its foundations, and to enforce its claims upon the whole Church.

The responsibility both of the initiation and carrying on of this terrible system rests upon the Popes alone. The new theory of the autocratic power of the Papacy needed some all-pervading agency—everywhere active, but nowhere conspicuous—that should subdue each opponent as he arose, strike dread into every soul, and put every complaining voice to silence, either in death or in a dungeon. And so, it was the Popes who began by compelling bishops and priests to condemn, those whom they now regarded as heterodox, to torture, confiscation of goods, imprisonment and death, and to enforce the execution of these sentences upon the civil authorities under pain of excommunication.

There was nothing in the literature of the time to pave the way for it. And it was not, until it had been systematized and carried out in many places that the schoolmen undertook its justification. Thomas Aquinas is its great defender.

When this tribunal was first established it was not intended that it should exceed the powers of punishment which had been for some time vested in the bishops. But in the hands of the Dominicans, to whom the Popes handed over its whole management, subject only to their approval, it soon manifested an independence and exercised an influence which were surprising. To disarm the bishops who were jealous at this new encroachment on their powers, the Popes ordered that they and the inquisitors should act jointly; but very soon, with the connivance of the Popes, the bishops were set aside, and the inquisitors acted independently of them. Then the secular powers were jealous because the property of criminals was formerly forfeited to the State, whereas now it would go directly to the Papal treasury. To avoid this difficulty the Popes decreed that the inquisitors should condemn, that the magistrate should execute the sentence, and that one-third of the property of the accused should be appropriated by the State, and that the other two-thirds should be equally divided between the inquisitors and the Pope. So that each of the parties concerned in conducting the trial had a direct and large pecuniary interest in securing the condemnation of the accused.

It is a terrible thing to say, but this conclusion is forced upon the student of the history of this dread tribunal that, whatever may have been its object at its first establishment, it was very soon transformed into a vast organized *system* of *murder*, carried on mainly for the sake of plunder, under the sanction and direction of the Papal court. The pontiffs took care to urge kings and princes to support, with the aid of their secular power, their emissaries in all their endeavours to extirpate heresy, and so well were their wishes responded to, that in a short time, no one, even of the most unblemished character and the greatest piety, could consider himself safe from being cruelly put to death, if he should happen not to have secured the favour of the inquisitors.

From the year 1200 to 1500 there are a long series of Papal ordinances on the Inquisition, of ever-increasing severity and cruelty; their whole policy towards what they call heresy runs on without a break. Every Pope confirms and improves upon the decrees of his predecessor. All is directed towards the one end, of uprooting every difference of belief. And very soon the principle came to be openly asserted that the mere thought of heresy, without having betrayed itself by any outward sign, was penal.

Nothing but the absolute dictation of the Popes and the conviction of their infallibility in all questions of religion and morals, which the forged decretals had embedded in the mind of Western Europe, could have made the Christian world, even of that day, silently, though sullenly, admit the code of the Inquisition—a code which contradicted the simplest principles of Christian justice and love to our neighbours, and which would have been rejected with universal horror by the ancient Catholic Church.

Besides the open profession of known heretical opinions there were sixteen offences enumerated which caused the persons guilty of them to be suspected of heresy and made them liable to the punishment of the Holy Office. These were certain kinds of blasphemy, sorcery and divination, the invocation of demons, to remain a year or longer under excommunication without asking for absolution, or performing the penance which had been imposed, schisms, favouring or concealing heretics, refusing to take the oath to drive heretics from their estates, the neglect of governors and kings to do the bidding of the Inquisition, the refusal to repeal statutes or decrees contrary to the measures of the Holy Office, for lawyers or other persons to assist heretics with their advice, or to conceal papers which would lead to their conviction, to give Christian burial to heretics, to refuse to take the oath in the trial of heretics ; in addition to these were deceased persons, who had been denounced as heretics and concerning whom the Popes had decreed that their bodies should be disinterred and burned, their property confiscated and their memory pronounced infamous, lastly Jews and Moors if they tried in any way to convert Catholics to their Faith.

When an inquisitor in his judicial rounds arrived in a town, he called upon the magistrate to put in force all the laws against heretics. He then announced that all who should voluntarily confess should receive absolution, and be subjected only to slight penances, but that those who should be denounced should be proceeded against with severity.

After a brief interval the informers were summoned, and proceedings were begun by a denunciation, or direct charge of heresy, made by some of these, or by information wrung from a prisoner under torture. Anonymous denunciations were received without scruple, and were acted on in the same manner as those given under the sanction of a name; and even the depositions of those refused a hearing in all other trials, either from personal enmity to the accused, or on account of public infamy, such as perjurers, panderers, and malefactors were admitted. It is needless to point out how this enabled those bearing a grudge to avenge themselves on their enemies in a most dastardly manner.

Many denunications were effected through confessors, who imposed it as a duty upon their penitents to make known to the Holy Office anything which they had seen or heard that was contrary to the Catholic faith, or to the Inquisition. Absolution was rigidly refused until the denunciation was effected, and it very frequently happened that a wife informed against her husband, a parent against a child, or a child against a parent. It is related of Blanco White, for instance, that his mother, who was a good Catholic, and was aware that he held opinions, which if known would subject him to the power of the inquisitors, would not dare to speak to him for days together, lest he should unguardedly give expression to those opinions; in which case she would, of course, be compelled by her confessor to denounce him to the Holy Office.

If the inquisitors thought the words or acts warranted enquiry, an inquest was commenced. The persons named in the denunciation as able to give testimony were summoned. Each witness was compelled to swear first that he would not divulge anything which he might see or hear. He was then asked, not concerning the particular case in which he had been summoned, but in general terms, whether he had ever seen or heard anything which was, or appeared to be contrary to the Catholic faith, or the rights of the Inquisition. Being ignorant of the object for which he was called, and knowing that he could only escape the torture by telling what he did know, he would generally divulge circumstances implicating persons not previously denounced. The inquisitors would then artfully set to work to weave a web of evidence that would lead to the conviction of those thus named. They would then draw out of the witnesses all they knew of the case in which they had been called, and as they did not know for what purpose they were required, nor even whether

G

they were to be treated as witnesses, or as accused men,
they were so terrified as to be altogether unmanned, and
often said things, and signed declarations which went far
beyond their knowledge or belief. The accused were never
confronted by the witnesses. They had no opportunity
of questioning them, or even of knowing who they were.
In cases where three persons conspired against the
accused, he was beyond all chance of escape, for the
accuser's evidence, and the concurring testimony of two
witnesses were enough to convict him. And, indeed, so
artfully were persons treated, and so impenetrable was
the secrecy in which inquisitors involved evidences and
witnesses alike, that it was almost a miracle if any person who was once accused established his innocence
against such odds. Only about one in 2,000 did escape.

If the evidence was thought sufficiently strong it was
submitted to appointed theologians, who had to determine
whether the accused were guilty of heresy or only
suspected of heresy; and if suspected, whether the
suspicion were light, grave, or violent. Justifiers, as
they were called, were often so profoundly ignorant of
systematic theology that they not unfrequently condemned, as heretical, the dogmas taught by the most
eminent Roman Catholic theologians.

As soon as anyone was arrested, all his property was
seized and retained to pay the expenses of his arrest and
the cost of his maintenance during his incarceration—if,
as rarely happened—he was released, the balance was
returned to him; but if condemned, it was added to the
funds of the tribunal.

Those against whom the charge of heresy was preferred
were always confined in a dark dungeon for forty-eight

hours without food or drink; sometimes they were locked up for weeks, sometimes for months, in the secret prisons, without even being informed of the cause of their arrest. These secret prisons, in the early history of the tribunal, were damp, filthy dungeons, unfit for the reception of human beings; latterly they were of a more wholesome character—small, but light and dry. Yet, with these advantages they were most frightful places of confinement. The most profound solitude and silence reigned. None entered within the walls without the certainty either of meeting a disgraceful and horrible death, at the stake, or, if life were spared, of being indelibly stigmatised and eternally lost in public opinion. The solitude, and the absence of all occupation, the contemplation of a fearful death, and the feeling that the convicted felon or the galley slave would be respected in society in comparison with him—all these would combine to precipitate the unhappy prisoner into despair too fearful to contemplate. Instances were by no means rare of men being imprisoned by the Holy Office who, when they entered, were men of strong constitutions and vigorous minds, but who, when they left its dungeons, had feeble bodies and minds entirely broken down by intense mental and bodily sufferings. Many of you will remember in Dickens' pictures from Italy his harrowing description of the inquisitorial prison which he saw in the Pope's palace at Avignon.

"A few steps," he says, "brought us to the dungeons in which the prisoners of the Inquisition were confined for forty-eight hours after their capture, without food or drink, that their constancy might be shaken, even before they were confronted with their gloomy judges. The day has not got in there yet. They are still, small cells, shut in by four unyielding, close, hard walls ; still profoundly dark, still massively doored and walled as of old. On we went into a vaulted chamber, now used as a storeroom, once the chapel of the Holy Office. The place where the tribunal sat was plain. The platform might have been removed but yesterday. Conceive the parable of the Good Shepherd having been painted on the wall of one of these Inquisition chambers ! But it was, and may be traced there yet.

" High up in the jealous walls are niches where the faltering replies of the accused were heard and noted down. Many of them had been brought out of the very cell we had just looked into. We had trodden in their very footsteps. Then into a room adjoining—a rugged room, with a funnel-shaped, contracting roof, open at the top to the bright day. The chamber of torture, and the roof was made of that shape to stifle the victim's cries. See the stone trough for the water-torture. Gurgle, swell, bloat, burst, heretic—for the Redeemer's honour. Suck the bloody rag, deep down into your unbelieving body, heretic, at every breath you draw. And know us, for His chosen servants, true believers in the Sermon on the Mount, elect disciples of Him who never did a miracle but to heal ; who never struck a man with palsy, blindness, deafness, dumbness, madness, or any one affection of mankind, and never stretched his blessed hands out but to give relief and ease. There the furnace was. There they made the irons red-hot. Those holes supported the sharp stake on which the tortured persons hung poised, dangling with their whole weight from the roof. A cold air laden with an earthy smell falls upon the face. It comes from a trapdoor in the wall. One looks in. Downward to the bottom, upward to the top of a a steep, dark, lofty tower, very dismal, very dark, very cold, the executioner flung those who were past all further torturing down here.

" Again, into the chapel of the Holy Office, a little trap door in the floor. Behold the oubliettes of the Inquisition, subterranean, black, terrible, deadly ; my blood ran cold as I looked down into the vaults where these forgotten creatures, with recollections of the world outside, of wives, friends, brothers, children—starved to death, and the stones rang with their unavailing groans. But the thrill I felt on seeing the accursed wall below, decayed and broken through, and the sun shining in through its gaping wounds, was like a sense of victory and triumph."

"Place yourself in imagination beneath the vault of yonder rugged room, picture to yourself the scene, and consider what unguessed-at misery it means. Begin by laying aside the thought of friends, from whom when once a prisoner, you are altogether severed. Not a soul of them will ever see you again. Not one can even conjecture where you are. You have been trapped, it may be, in a lonely street, and brought hither in the dead of night. In another ten minutes you must undergo the question. What answer will you give ? Will you confess to these men after the example of St. Paul : " After the way which ye call heresy, so worship I the God of my fathers." Or will you deny your own convictions, and profess to believe what you do not believe. To do this will secure for you, at the least an easy death, instead of a death by fire,

possibly no more than a short penance, possibly seclusion
in some well-known monastery. But if you will denounce
your friends and enter the service of your tormentors as
a spy, you will gain for yourself, not only life, but much
that makes life luxurious, if not splendid. Remember, if
you choose against this, you will go down into silence.
" No protest of yours, no word nor deed will ever be
known; neither the fact of your death, if you die, nor
yet of your existence, if you should continue to live in
any other vocation than the abhorred one of being a spy
upon your friends." Such was the policy of this accursed
tribunal (Jackson on Retribution). Will you not, my
brethren, lift up your hearts in thankfulness to God now
that he has not subjected you to such an ordeal.

When the prisoner was brought before his judges, he
was not informed of the charges against him, but was exhorted to speak the truth and confess whatever he had
said or done against the Catholic faith or the Inquisition.
After three audiences of this kind, the prosecutor or fiscal,
as he was called, formulated his charges, and instead of
reducing them to proper heads, he multiplied the number
of charges, in proportion to the number of witnesses who
had testified against him. Thus supposing a certain conversation to have been reported by five or six witnesses,
with the inevitable variations, five or six different accusations, instead of one were framed upon their evidence.
These accusations were read at his public punishment in
an *auto da fe*, without any diminution of their number,
and the ignorant mob were led to applaud the leniency of
the Holy Office, which had awarded so light a punishment
to a criminal guilty of such a large number of heinous
crimes.

When the farce of these examinations was over, all were alike subjected to torture, whether they had confessed their guilt or denied it. The former was tortured, not for the crime he had confessed, but that he might be compelled to confess other crimes of which the Holy Office was not cognisant, and those who had either denied or partially confessed their guilt were tortured, that the former might be compelled to confess something, and the latter to acknowledge more than he had already done.

This torture was of such a dreadful character, that death often resulted from its infliction. A law was therefore passed forbidding it to be inflicted more than once, but with their usual fiendish ingenuity the inquisitors evaded this law. They had a physician present who informed them when it could no longer be continued without danger of life, and then the torture was declared to be commenced, but not terminated, and the wretched sufferer was sent back to his dungeon with the comfortable assurance that the punishment would be re-inflicted so soon as his frame was capable of bearing it. It very often happened that victims who were wholly innocent of the charge laid against them were simply bullied and tortured into admitting what the inquisitors wished them to admit, in order to shorten their pangs.

That the screams of the prisoners might not be heard, the torture was inflicted in the hall of torture, as Dickens describes it.

The first torture was that of the pulley. The hands were tied behind the back and a heavy weight attached to the feet; then the victim was suddenly hoisted to the ceiling by a rope attached to his hands and running through a pulley. The arms were thus wrenched from their sockets, and while thus suspended the prisoner was often whipped; at other times had a red-hot iron thrust into various parts of his body, and he was coldly admonished by the inquisitors to speak the truth. If he refused to confess and his arms had not been dislocated, he was suddenly dropped to within a few feet of the ground and brought up with a jerk which seldom failed to accomplish that result.

If he still refused to confess he was subjected, as soon as the physician pronounced him strong enough, to the torture of the fire or chafing-dish. The prisoner was placed in iron stocks so that he could not move hand or foot, a chafing-dish full of burning charcoal was brought; his feet, being frequently rubbed with grease, were literally fried. During the process he was exhorted to confess. If by the extremity of pain he promised to do so, the attendants introduced a board between his feet and the fire, and he was required to go on with his confession. If he did not do so the board was withdrawn and the process went on.

Another torture was the rack. Though there were several machines bearing that name, the simplest drew the arms in opposite directions till torn from their sockets.

Another was a trough with rungs across the middle of the victims back, his arms and legs were tied to the sides with ropes. These were to be tightened by turn after turn of sticks till the ropes cut into the flesh,—often to the bones. But as if this diabolical cruelty were not enough, the prisoner's nose was stopped so that he could not breathe through it, and a linen bag was first inserted into his throat and water poured in. In his desperate efforts to draw breath the prisoner often burst a blood vessel and died under the infliction. If the prisoner could bear it, cords were tied to his toes, and he was strung up to the ceiling till he fainted. The tortures varied, but were of every conceivable description that fiendish cruelty could invent. Women, who were frequently the victims of the Holy Office, were treated in the most immodest and brutal manner.

Upon the evidence thus obtained the charges were formulated. The accused, as soon as he was able to appear, was brought before his judges. The charges were read over, one by one, and to each he was required to give an immediate answer. This was intended most unfairly to entrap him into statements and admissions which would make it impossible for him to defend himself against the charges yet to be made, of which he was in utter ignorance. All means of legal protection were withheld from him; there was no right of appeal and no legal adviser allowed him. Any lawyer who undertook his defence would have been himself excommunicated and summoned before the tribunal.

Those acquitted, averaging about one in 2,000 of the accused, were allowed to return to their homes and families with certificates of absolution; but no reparation was made for the loss of health, honour, or property, nor were the names of false witnesses who had procured their denunciation given up. The rest were condemned either to be reconciled, after appearing in the *auto da fe*, and fulfilling their penance, which meant often years of imprisonment in a dungeon, or as a galley slave, or they were burnt to ashes at the stake.

When sentence had once been pronounced no one could plead or supplicate on behalf of the heretic. Breach of this law, even when the petitioner was a wife pleading for her husband, or a parent for his child, involved the supplicant in the guilt of the accused.

This devilish enactment comes from the brain of the canonized monster, Pope Pius V.

The inquisitor was forbidden to show any pity. Torture in its most terrible form was the usual way of extorting confession. No recantation or confession of orthodoxy could save the accused; he was allowed confession, absolution, and communion, and his profession of repentance was accepted *in foro sacramenti*, but he was told at the same time that it would not be accepted judicially, and he must die if he were a relapsed heretic. Lastly, to fill up the measure of iniquity, his innocent family was deprived of its property by legal confiscation. Life only, said Innocent III., was to be left to the sons of misbelievers, and that only as an act of mercy. They were therefore made incapable of all civil offices and dignities.

The pretext that was put forth for the formal establishment of the Inquisition was that it was needed to uproot and exterminate the fugitive Waldenses and Albigenses who, after their land had been desolated by the crusaders the Popes sent against them, were hunted like wild beasts from their own country, and sought to hide themselves in Northern Italy, Switzerland, Spain, Venice and Hungary.

One cannot study their history without feeling that their chief offence was that they refused to accept the new doctrine about the Pope's supremacy. Tens of thousands of them were seized and subjected to the terrible tortures and death of the Inquisition.

That we may form some idea of the terrible work of this tribunal, let me mention a few facts. In the first eighteen years of the Spanish Inquisition under Torquamada 10,220 persons were burnt, and 97,321 imprisoned, banished and reduced to want. During the rule of one, Chief Inquisitor Diaz, 38,440 persons were condemned by it in Spain alone, 2,598 of them were burnt. During the brief rule of his mild successor, Cisneros, Llorente estimates the number of victims at 3,564 burnt, and 48,059 condemned to various other punishments. Pope Adrian VI. was Inquisitor General of Spain for five years before he became Pope, and during that time the number of those condemned was 28,220, of whom 1,344 were burnt. He was succeeded by Marquinez, under whom 15,625 persons were condemned, of whom 2,250 were burnt. And so it went on century after century for five hundred years. And this, remember, only represents the havoc wrought in the one kingdom of Spain. The operations of the Inquisition were no doubt carried on in that land in the most systematic and wholesale manner. But its iron grasp was felt in every corner of the Western Empire. In Italy and Venice, and France, and Germany, and England, in Portugal and the Netherlands. In Mexico, in South America it rioted with unrestrained license. In India, China and Japan tens of thousands of victims, men, women and children, were doomed to infamy and death by this merciless tribunal. 1t bathed the kingdom of Poland in flames and blood. The Inquisition established by the Emperor Charles V. in the Netherlands, for the extirpation of the followers of Luther, burnt more than fifty thousand victims in that one small kingdom before this great king, in sheer disgust, flung off his imperial crown, and fled to hide himself from men in the solitude of St. Just. Our own Wm. Tindale, one of the early translators of the Bible into English, who had fled to the Netherlands for protection, was one of this number. Motley (Revolt of the Netherlands) estimates that probably not less than 100,000 victims of the Inquisition were burnt, strangled or buried alive during this reign, and this before Philip the Second began his fiercer and more sweeping measures. Pope Pius V. not only plotted with Rudolfi the assassination of Queen Elizabeth, but sent the consecrated hat and sword of honour to the monster Duke of Alva, the instrument of that fierceness, and as a reward for his savage cruelties in the Low Countries.

Dr. Dollinger says that the Reformation movement swept at least two-thirds of the entire population of Germany, France, Austria, and Italy out of the Roman obedience—and that it was reduced to its present diminished proportions largely by the wild extravagances of many of its leaders—but largely, also, by the religious wars which the Popes provoked, and by the merciless exercise of this dread tribunal. The first wholesale victims of the Inquisition were the Waldenses and Albigenses. The confiscation of their lands and goods gave the inquisitors their first taste of plunder. Very soon measures were devised for bringing the Jews, who were the wealthy business men of that time, under the grasp of the Holy Office. First they were compelled to choose between accepting Christian baptism or banishment and confiscation of goods. Many, to save their homes and fortunes, professed to be converted. They then became subject to suspicion of heresy as Catholic Christians. No profession or protestation could save them. They were hunted and imprisoned by thousands, their goods being invariably confiscated. They supplied for a long time a rich mine for the inquisitors to work.

When they were exhausted and well nigh exterminated, the Moors, who had lived in Spain for seven hundred years, and were the most intelllectual, learned, scientific, and successful citizens of the kingdom, were subjected to the same treatment as the Jews had been, until after years of merciless persecution the whole Moorish population were, by the machinations of the Chief Inquisitor, expelled and deported from Spain to Africa. Numbers were shipwrecked and drowned; many were murdered at sea for the sake of obtaining their property. The Spanish historians give details of men murdered in the presence of their wives and children; of children thrown overboard alive, of women violated, only to meet with the same fate a few days afterwards, details which can only be equalled by the most terrible instances in the annals of piracy. Of those who landed in Africa many were attacked by wandering Arabs, and slain; others perished of hunger and fatigue. Of six thousand persons who set out from Oran for Algiers, only one reached that city. While of 140,000 who set out for Africa about this time, 100,000 are believed by competent authorities to have perished within a month or two after their expulsion. Over a million of the most industrious and wealthy subjects of Spain were thus expelled or slain. And to that expulsion may be distinctly traced the beginning of the decline and fall of the once mighty Spanish empire. The Inquisition was directly concerned in this monstrous cruelty, inasmuch as their expulsion was devised and pressed upon the King by the Inquisitor-General, and was directly and indirectly assisted by the violent persecutions of that tribunal, the cruelties of which stirred up an inveterate hatred among the Moors against a religion which could tolerate such enormities. This monstrous outrage on humanity was, of course, accompanied by the confiscation of all the goods and property of the expelled.

I will conclude with one or two personal narratives out of the thousands that throng the histories of these times. In 1549, Constantine Fuenta, preacher to Charles V., was accused of Lutheranism. Before his arrest he had entrusted some of his MS. to a widow named Martinez, and she secreted them in a wall in the cellar of her house. She, too, was arrested for Lutheranism, and her property confiscated. Her son had concealed some of her property before the inventory was taken—the officer of the Inquisition came to him, and demanded the effects which he had concealed. He having no doubt that his mother had acknowledged the concealment of the books gave them up. On their evidence Fuenta was convicted of heresy, and thrown into a deep, dark, and damp dungeon, where the noxious vapours soon ended his sufferings. His goods were conficated, his effigy burnt, his memory pronounced infamous, and the inquisitors gave out that he had committed suicide.

Nicholas Burton, a native of Bristol, was burnt in an *auto da fe*. He went out with a cargo, which he pretended was his own; he was accused of Lutheranism, his property was confiscated, and he himself was burnt. John Fenton, the real owner of the cargo, went to Seville, and applied to the Inquisition to have his property restored. After being subjected to great expense and delay, they promised to restore his goods. In the meantime, however, they caused a charge to be laid against him of being a Lutheran. He barely escaped death, but his property was confiscated, and he was condemned to wear the sanbanito for a year.

Jane Bohorgues, a married woman near confinement, charged with the same offence, was tortured in the most brutal manner. In her feeble and forlorn condition, her child when born was torn from her, and before her strength would allow she was again subjected to the torture with the most feindish cruelty. The cords which bound her limbs penetrated to the bones, and caused the bursting of several blood-vessels. Blood flowed from her mouth in torrents, and she was carried back to her dungeon where she soon expired.

In 1704, Elizabeth Chaffer, who married Doctor Vasconcellos, a native of Maderia, remained faithful to the Church of England. During her husband's absence in Brazil, she had a dangerous sickness, and was informed on her recovery that she had been received into the Roman Church. She repudiated the ceremony, and was imprisoned for seven months, and then prosecuted for holding heretical opinions. Then she was sent a prisoner to the Inquisition of Lisbon. They appropriated all her money and jewellery, and then locked her up for nine months and fifteen days in a small dark room, about five feet square, on the ground floor. She was kept for most of the time on bread and water, and had nothing but a bundle of damp straw to sleep on. As she refused to conform, her back was stripped and lashed with a whip of knotted cords. Then they burnt her breast to the bone in three different places. After a month she received another severe whipping, and was then asked whether she would profess the Roman faith or be burnt. She resolutely refused to make the profession they required. She was told that the mercy of the tribunal was extended to endeavour to rescue her from the flames of hell, but that if her resolution was to burn rather than embrace the Roman Catholic religion, they would give her a trial of it before hand. She was then bound, so that she could not offer any resistance—her left foot was then made bare, and an iron slipper, red-hot, was fastened on her foot till the flesh was burnt away to the bone. As she fainted away the slipper was removed, and she was carried back to her dungeon. After a time, she was again whipped so cruelly that her back was torn all over. She was threatened with worse treatment still. And being quite unable to endure such a life of misery, she signed a paper of recantation and adhesion. She was then, after a time, dismissed in a most destitute condition, without any of her goods, or plate, or money being restored to her.

Wm. Lithgow, a Scotch traveller who had gone over Europe, arrived in Spain in 1620; he was seized and imprisoned as a suspected spy by the inquisitors. He has written a harrowing description of the prison, surpassing

that of Dickens' in its actual horrors. He was subjected
to every one of the different kinds of torture I have described, and others more revolting still. Lithgow was
accidentally discovered by some English factors, who secured his release. On his arrival in England in 1621,
James the I. went to see him, and a long diplomatic corres-
pondence grew out of his treatment.

These are only a few instances picked at random out of
thousands. Had I time, I could adduce well attested
proofs, the narratives of those who endured or witnessed
the inflictions, of the truth of every statement I have
made, and of every description I have given of this frightful tribunal. No one can read its history without feeling
that for its inconceivable cruelties, its wholesale murders
perpetrated in the name of religion, and under the direct
authority of the Pope, there must be a mighty retribution
in store for the Roman Church yet. Other Christians
taught by her foul example. The Church of England, the
Presbyterians, the Congregationalists have persecuted one
another cruelly—but they are one and all deeply ashamed
of their conduct—have repented of their sin, and repudiated it. But the Roman Church stands formally committed
to this frightful policy still. For this accursed system is part
to the actual ecclesiastical code of the Roman Church at this
moment, no scrap of it having been ever withdrawn, re-
pealed, or modified, though power to enforce it is happily
lacking. And it is probable that the Vatican decrees have
made its repeal now forever impossible.

I cannot dwell upon the practical reflections which such
a recital suggests. It must make us shudder at the revelation it gives us of the power of evil. That men could be

H

found capable of such hard-heartedness, such treachery, such fiendish cruelty, surpasses imagination. It was however perpetrated in the name of truth, and at first with the intention of upholding what they believed to be the truth. Do not think that the powers which instigated this monstrous wickedness have ceased to be. They are carrying on their warfare with different weapons now, using the very abhorrence which men feel for the methods then employed in the name of truth, to make the truth itself odious and men indifferent about truth altogether.

Extracts made by Littledale from the Sacro Arsanle of Bolonga 1665, a hand book of the procedure of the Inquisition.

CXXVI. Torture should begin with those most suspected, and if they be man and woman, is to begin with the woman, as the more timid and frail : and if all are males then with the youngest and feeblest.

CCIV. The sons of heretics do not incur the penalties enacted against them, provided they judiciously disclose to the Holy Tribunal the heresy of their parents and secure their imprisonment.

CCXXI. A true Catholic is bound to denounce heretics, even if he have promised, pledged his faith, and sworn to them not to disclose them ; such promise or oath being of no force or obligation.

CCXXXIV. The Doctors (and with good reason) hold the crime of heresy as so atrocious that they account heresy incurred through ignorance, as worse than murder committed with treachery.

CCXXXVI. If heretics have Catholic children, nevertheless their goods are to be confiscated, and no regard is to be had of the chrildren.

LECTURE VII.

ROMAN DEPARTURE FROM CATHOLIC DOCTRINES AND PRACTICE.

"It was needful for me to write unto you, and exhort you that you should earnestly contend for the faith which was once delivered unto the saints."—Jude, 3.

IT is a duty to examine with unceasing care the spaciousness, and beauty, and strength, and structure of the Church of God, that we may be able to defend and maintain it, and may hand on to the generations to come a true conception and description of the Divine architecture. The words of the text call us to another duty: to contend with all our might for the propagation and preservation of the deposit of truth, the faith—the definite, revealed doctrines that have been entrusted to the Church as the pillar and ground of the truth, to witness to and to keep. There is danger, as we have seen, of unhallowed hands meddling with the Ark of God, the outward structure, and changing and overturning the divinely-appointed constitution of the one body. There is danger of indolent minds holding the truth in unrighteousness, of impure minds corrupting the faith, of unbelieving minds subverting it altogether. Against each tendency in ourselves, and in others, we are here bidden earnestly to contend. I have given proof enough already that the Roman Church has fallen into the snare first named, and that she differs widely—one fears almost fatally—from the divinely-constituted order and harmony of the primitive Catholic Church. By a law of unbending sequence, as history seems unquestionably to indicate, she has fallen into the second snare as well, and has corrupted, overloaded, and obscured the faith once for all delivered to the saints.

I intend to invite your attention to two or three points —I cannot cover the whole field—in which the Roman Church differs from the Catholic Church in doctrine and in practice. We saw last Sunday that it was the climbing ambition, the greedy lust for worldly wealth and influence, by which whole generations of Popes were possessed that led them to labour on with unscrupulous persistency and unceasing toil till they had, at least largely, succeeded in subverting the primitive constitution and government of the Catholic Church. It was precisely the same greed of power that led them to tamper with the Catholic faith, and to debase the worship of the Catholic Church by the allowance of heathen sentiments and practices. This grew naturally out of the consuming desire of the Roman Pontiffs to extend at first their patriarchal and appellate jurisdiction, which brought them in large revenues, and then to extend the Papal sovereignty— when that idea was conceived—over the whole Church.

In order to conciliate the heathen, and make it easy to

induce whole tribes and nations to enter the Church of the Roman obedience, heathen customs and sentiments were winked at, or openly allowed. This is no fancy of my own. It rests upon the very substantial authority of Pope Gregory the Great. In instructing Augustine of Canterbury how to act towards his Saxon converts, he says, "Let this be done: as these people have been in the habit of slaying many cattle in the sacrifices to their demons, so for their sakes ought there to be some solemnity, the object of it only being changed. Then, upon a dedication or upon the nativity of some of the holy martyrs   *   *   *   let it be permitted to make arbours with the branches of trees round what once were but heathen temples. Then celebrate such solemnities with religious feasts so that the people will not immolate animals to demons, but slay them and partake of them with thanks and praises to God.   *   *   *   For be it remembered that it is not possible to deprive those whose minds are hardened of all things." And then, in justification of his advice, he says: "When the Lord made Himself known to the people of Israel in Egypt, He still reserved for His own use the sacrifices which it had been accustomed to tender to the demons, and even commanded them to immolate animals in His honour, so that as their hearts changed they would lose one portion of the sacrifice; that whilst the animals were immolated as they had been immolated, yet being offered to God and not to idols, the sacrifices may no longer be the same." The advice with the illustration—of very questionable theology—shows that it was the policy of Rome, even at that early day, to minimise in the minds of the heathen the extent of the change they would have to make in becoming Christians, and so to conciliate them by retaining many of their customs. The same spirit controlled the whole action of the Roman Church with regard to the worship of images, angels, saints, and relics.

One of the most frequent reproaches flung at the early Christians by the heathen was that they had no images among them or in their places of worship (C. Cels., viii., 17.) Cæcilius (Ap. Minuc. F. p. 19), asks, Why have they no known images ? And so Arnobius (L. vi.) says to the heathen, Ye are wont to charge us with the greatest impiety that we set up no images or likenesses of the gods. The statements of Origen, Tertullian and Minucius attest beyond all dispute that images of every kind were utterly disallowed in the Church of their day. The Benedictine (Roman Catholic) editors of Origen sum up the principles of the early Christians in this brief sentence : " They held that no image of God was to be made." " What avail images ? " asks Tertullian, " which are the monuments either of the dead or of the absent ? " St. Augustine denies that Christians had images in their churches. (Im. pp. 113, 6.) The testimony of the whole primitive Church is ovewhelmingly against the worship of images. Even Pope Gregory writes to Serenius, Bishop of Marseilles, that he had heard that Serenius, seeing certain persons worshipping images, had broken those same images in the Church and cast them out, and says : " I praise you in this that nothing made with hands should be worshipped." He then draws a distinction between the use of pictures, as a means of instructing the unlettered (just as they are used in our Sunday-schools now), and the abuse of worshipping them, and advises that they be retained to the former end, and care be taken that the people sin not in worshipping the picture.

This advice was widely acted upon ; and so, under the plea of conciliating the heathen on the one hand, and of instructing the ignorant on the other, the system of venerating images grew to such excess in the eighth century that three emperors, Leo the Isaurian, Constantine 'Copronymus, and Leo IV., took measures for removing images from churches, and suppressing image worship by force. These measures were strongly opposed by Popes Gregory II. and III., who stirred up rebellion against the emperors, and so Constantine assembled a Council at Constantinople in 754, which declared that all worship of images was contrary to Scripture and the sense of the Church in the purer ages ; that it was idolatry, and forbidden by the Second Commandment. They also maintained that the use of images in churches was a custom borrowed from the Pagans ; that it was of dangerous tendency, and ought to be abolished. But in the year 780 the Empress Irene succeeded to the control of the Eastern Empire, and entered into league with Pope Adrian. They held another council at Nice, to which only bishops favouring the use of images were invited. This council decreed that the cross, the images of Christ, Mary, the angels and the saints were entitled to the worship of veneration; yet that they were not entitled to Divine worship, Latria, properly so called.

The report of the proceedings of this Council, though approved by the Pope, kindled a flame of furious opposition throughout the Churches of the West. The English

Church, under the guidance of the learned Alcuin, led the
way, and at the Council of Verulam (St. Albans), 793,
denounced the image worship which this Eastern Council
had sanctioned " as a thing which the Church of God
utterly abhors." In the next year the great Council of
Frankfort was held at the summons of the Emperor
Charlemagne. It represented the whole Western Church,
England, France, Germany, Spain and Italy, including
legates from the Pope, and it condemned as " execrable
in the Church of God all worship, adoration and service
of images." And so the Council of Paris, in 824, in discussing this subject, denounced the absurdities of Pope
Adrian, who, they say, " had commanded an heretical
worship of images." Thus the whole Western Church
formally and emphatically reject the doctrines of the
pseudo Nicene Council, and declare what up to that time
had been the doctrine and practice of the Catholic Church.
And that decision stands unreversed to this day as the
law of the Western Church.

In spite, however, of this formal rejection, this heathen
superstition revived amongst the half-instructed converts
from heathenism, and grew apace, just as the Papal power
grew, until it absorbed very largely the devotions of the
people. I am aware that Roman Catholic controversialists deny that any real worship is paid to images, and
that they are merely regarded as edifying memorials of
those whom they represent. But when we know that
the common people are taught to bow down before sta-
tues and pictures of our blessed Saviour, of His virgin
mother, and of His saints and angels, though we are told
that they make no prayers to the images, but to those of

which they are images, yet, we ask, wherein does such
worship differ from idolatry ?   The heathen, as we learn
from St. Augustine, protested that they did not pray to
the image, but to the god whom the image was meant to
represent. So that the very essence of idolatry is to worship God through the medium of an image or representation.   It is against this very sin that the second commandment is directed ; and it is no doubt the conscious-
ness of this fact, whatever explanations may be offered,
that lies at the root of the Roman mode of teaching the
commandments so as to slip the second commandment
altogether out of sight.   And so it comes to pass that not
one Roman Catholic in a million knows or is taught that
image worship is sinful and can be abused.   Nay, eminent Roman divines have taught unchecked that to the
very images of Christ was due the same supreme worship
which is due to Christ Himself, even that Latria with
which none but the Holy Trinity and the Incarnate Word
must be approached.   Bellarmine, who himself took a
hesitating course and held that Latria was only improperly
and by accident due to an image, yet tells us that the
opposite opinion was held by Thomas Aquinas, Cajetan,
and Bonaventura, and he himself says that " the images
of Christ and the saints are to be venerated, not only by
accident and improperly, but also by themselves properly ;
so that themselves terminate the veneration as in themselves considered, and not only as they take the place of
their examples."

Azorius, the Jesuit, says that the image is to be honoured
and worshipped with the same honour and worship as that
with which he is worshipped whose the image is. (So.

Azor. Just., Mort. Tom., 1 Let. ix., c. 9.) And Thomas
Aquinas says, " The same reverence should be displayed
towards an image of Christ as towards Christ Himself ;
and seeing that Christ is adored with the adoration of
Latria (*i. e.* supreme religious worship) it follows that His
image is to be adored with the adoration of Latria.
(Summa. ii., xxv., 3.) Again, the cross is adored with the
same adoration as Christ, that is with adoration of Latria,
and for that reason we address and supplicate the cross
just as we do the Crucified Himself." If this be not to
break God's commandments and teach men so, then it is
hard to see how God's commandments can be broken.
Even the enlightened heathen seldom went so far as to
believe the worship due properly to the idol itself, and
not merely to its original and prototype. Roman Catholics
insist that there is no idolatry in this teaching and practice. It may be so ; but if so, it is quite impossible to
tell what the term idolatry means. At all events, we see
plainly enough from the quotations given that the Roman
Church of to-day differs very widely on this subject both
from the doctrine and practice of the Catholic Church of
the first eight centuries.

It is just the same with the history of the great crying
crime of the practical system of the Roman Church—her
obscuration, nay, overthrow, of faith in Jesus Christ as
our only Mediator and Redeemer—the cultus, they call it,
of the blessed Virgin. It has no place whatever in the
faith or practice of the Catholic Church of the first ages.
The first approaches to it are rejected with almost furious
indignation by the great Church teachers. The vast majority of the Christian writers before the Council of Nice

whose writings have come down to us, in all their historical, doctrinal, and devotional statements never mention
the blessed Virgin in any way whatever. Of the few
who do refer to her in an historical way not one directs
any devotion to be paid to her, or assigns her any other
place than that of being the honoured instrument of the
Saviour's incarnation. Two, Origen and Tertullian, blame
her for entertaining unbelieving doubts. Irenæus says
that St. Mary's obedience counterbalances Eve's disobedience, so that she has become the advocate of Eve. We
have only a barbarous Latin translation of what he wrote
and it is evident that he is not thinking of the blessed
Virgin as the advocate of Eve in the active sense of
pleading for her now, but only of the one act of her ready
submission to the divine will, as furnishing a counter-
balancing plea to the disobedience of Eve. And it is evident that he had no notion of the Roman doctrine concerning the Virgin mother, for in another place he speaks
of Christ having checked the unreasonable haste of His
mother at Cana. (Adv. Haer. iii., xvi.) There is no
change in the testimony of the greatest fathers even after
Nice. In their catechisms, prepared for the instruction
of the people, there is absolute silence as to any religious
homage due to her, and in their devotional utterances
there is nothing that can be tortured into an address to
her of any kind. St. Chrysostom does not hesitate to say
that she was ignorant of the full mystery of the incarnation, and that she was moved by ambition and arrogance
in sending that message to her son. (Hom. on St. Matt.
xii., 48.) St. Basil speaks of her as wavering in belief at
the time of the Passion. (Epist. 260.)

St. Gregory Nyssen says nothing created is to be worshipped by man.   *   *   *   "We who are taught by the Scriptures to look to the true Godhead are instructed to regard every created being as foreign from the Divine nature, and to serve and reverence the uncreated nature alone." (Contra Eunomium.) (St. Ephanius, 403), a Doctor, says, Mary's body was holy, indeed, but she was not a Deity. She was a virgin, too, and honoured, but not given to us for worship. And he concludes, " Christ called her woman, as in prophecy, because of the heresies and schisms which were to come upon the earth, lest any one, through excessive adoration for that holy Virgin, should fall into the silly nonsense of that heresy (that of the Collyrideans).   *   *   *   For if Christ willeth not that the angels should be worshipped, how much more is He unwilling that worship should be paid to her who is born of Anna ? Let Mary be honoured ; but let the Father, Son, and. Holy Ghost alone be worshipped. Let no one worship Mary." He says that this idolatrous heresy has only for its promoters weak, fickle, narrow-minded women, prone to error, and that they must be put to silence. " With these agree St. Jerome, Doctor, 478 ; St. Augustine, Doctor, 430 ; St. Cyril, of Alexandria, 440. And, finally, nothing whatever implying this cultus is to be found in the copious writings either of Pope Leo the Great, 461, or of Pope Gregory the Great, 604. And when we first find the cultus of the blessed Virgin, or of the angels, making its appearance, it is at once challenged and condemned as a novel heresy." (Littledale.)

Such was the doctrine, such the practice of the Catholic Church for over 600 years with regard to the cultus of the blessed Virgin.   Like the worship of angels, images, and relics, it was introduced to conciliate the heathen, and it found a soil ready prepared in the minds of those barbarous hordes who had been accustomed to worship the Queen of Heaven and her attendants or rivals.   And so this custom which the fathers rejected with abhorrence as an idolatrous heresy grew apace in that soil till it reached at last its truly appalling proportions in the modern Roman Church.

I have not time to trace its history, but invite your attention to a few illustrations of the accredited Roman teaching on the subject now.   One of their most learned writers, Suarez, says "it is a universal sentiment in the Roman Church that the intercession of Mary is not only useful, but in a certain manner necessary, because God has determined to give us no grace except through the hands of Mary."   And so it is taught in authorized books that " it is morally impossible for those to be saved who neglect the devotion of the blessed Virgin ; " that " it is the will of God that all graces should pass through her hands ; " that "no creature obtained any grace from God save according to the dispensation of His holy mother," (quoted from Bernerdine by Liguori).   That Jesus has in fact said "no one shall be partaker of my blood except through the intercession of My mother."   That " our salvation is in her hands."   That " it is impossible for any to be saved who turns away from her, or is disregarded by her."   That " God Himself is subject to the command of Mary."   That " God has resigned into her hands His omnipotence in the sphere of grace."   That "it is safer to seek salvation through her than directly from Jesus.   It was necessary that Christ should constitute His well-beloved mother a mediator between us and Him, that she would appease the wrath of her Son." (Iac de Valent en Eupos Magni.) Again, it is taught that "God retained justice unto Himself and granted mercy to her;" "that she is the throne of grace whereof the Apostle speaketh to which we are to come;" "that she appeaseth the just anger of her Son;" "she is the only refuge of those who have incurred the Divine indignation." (Blosius in Glories of Mary, p. 93.) And these are not the mere opinions of private teachers, but of Doctors whose teaching has been examined and approved, of authorised books of devotion and instruction, nay, of Popes themselves, e. g : "On this hope," says Pius IX., "we chiefly rely that the most blessed Virgin,   *   *   who by the foot of virtue bruised the serpent's head, and who, being constituted between Christ and His Church,   *   *   hath ever delivered the Christian people from calamities of all sorts. For ye know very well, venerable brethren, that the whole of our confidence is placed in the most holy Virgin, since God has placed in Mary the fulness of all good, that accordingly, we may know that if there is any hope in us, if any grace, if any salvation, it redounds to us from her, because such is His will who has willed that we should have everything through Mary." (Ep. Encycl., 1849.)

That is the way the last Pope interpreted and taught this doctrine. We have been told that the present occupant of the Papal throne is a liberal and enlightened man, who has no sympathy with the superstitions of his predecessor. And yet who of us has not been horrified at the pure and simple heathenism that pervades every line

of that encyclical of his published about a month ago,
calling the faithful to observe a novenna to the blessed
Virgin, and promising all sorts of indulgences for the mere
mechanical recitation of prayers to her ?   Neither the
name nor the doctrine of Christ has the faintest recognition.   It is in fact an entire endorsation of Liguorian
teaching about Mary.   Again, De Salazar (pp. 621-629),
hesitates not to say that " Mary loved the world and gave
her only begotten Son for it ; for with priestly piety she
offered Him up as a sacrifice for the world.   Many things
are asked from God and are not granted ; they are asked
from Mary and are obtained."   " At the command of the
Virgin all things obey, even God."   " The salvation of all
depends upon their being favoured and protected by Mary ;
he who is protected by Mary will be saved ; he who is
not will be lost.   Mary has only to speak and her Son
executes all."   (Glories of Mary, Liguori.)   That is what
is taught the people in the popular manuals of devotion
and instruction.

Think of this prayer in the Recolta, to be used during
the celebration of the mass : " I acknowledge thee and I
venerate thee, most holy Virgin, Queen of Heaven, Lady
Mistress of the universe, as daughter of the Eternal Father,
mother of His well-beloved Son, and most loving spouse
of the Holy Spirit ; kneeling at the feet of thy great
majesty with all humility, I pray through thy divine
charity wherewith thou wast so bounteously enriched on
thine assumption into heaven to vouchsafe me favour and
pity, placing me under thy most safe and faithful protection and receiving me into the number of those happy
and highly favoured servants of thine whose names thou

dost carry graven upon thy virgin heart." And think of this prayer published at Rome with license of Superiors in 1825 : " I adore you, Eternal Father ; I adore you, Eternal Son ; I adore you, most Holy Spirit ; I adore you, most holy Virgin, Queen of the heavens, lady and mistress of the universe." She is thus put on a virtual level with God as an object of worship, and as far as language can do it is honoured above Him. Salazar calls her "the complement of the whole Trinity, with body and soul under the sacred species." I shudder even to read what follows. Dr. Pusey (Enenicon) says there exists among the poor people of Rome a belief that in the Holy Eucharist not only our Lord but His mother is present. And the belief is defended by Oswald, one of their distinguished writers. (Dogmat. Mariol, p. 177.) " We maintain," he says, " a co-presence of Mary in the Eucharist. This is a necessary inference from our Marian theory, and we shrink back from no consequence. We are much inclined," he says afterwards, " to believe in an essential co-presence of Mary in her whole person." The same doctrine was stated long before by one of Rome's most careful commentators on Holy Scripture, Cornelius a Lapide, Eccl. xxiv., 29 : " As often as we eat the flesh of Christ in the holy Eucharist, so often do we in it really eat the flesh of the blessed Virgin." " As, then, we daily hunger after the flesh of Christ in the Eucharist, so, too, do we hunger for the same flesh of the blessed Virgin ; that we may drink her virgin endowments and ways and incorporate them into ourselves ; and this do not only priests and religious, but all Christians ; for the blessed Virgin feeds all with her own flesh, equally with the flesh of Christ, in the holy Eucharist."

Salazar says that St. Ignatius taught in a meditation that in the Eucharist he received not only the flesh and blood of Christ, but also a part, yea, a chief part of Mary. And Faber (pp. 29, 30, pre. Bld.) says, " There is some portion of the precious blood which was once Mary's own blood." And he says that Christ showed to St. Ignatius the very part of the host which had once belonged to the substance of Mary." I could multiply quotations of this kind vastly, but my soul is sick. If this teaching is not idolatry, if it is not barefaced, unmeasured blasphemy under the guise of religion, then I don't know the meaning of human speech. It was with reference to these statements that Dr. Newman said, when Dr. Pusey pressed them upon him, " they are like a bad dream ; they amaze, they terrify me."

I had intended in this lecture to point out that the Roman doctrine of purgatory, with its monstrous mass traffic, has a similar history, and is equally a departure from Catholic doctrine and practice; but I must not detain you longer. I will only say that not only does the Roman Church differ from the Catholic Church as to these doctrines and practices which we have been considering, but that her present attitude, both in teaching and practice, amounts to an absolute revolution in the Christian faith. It is not a gloss, or a development, or a modification, but a radical change. Theoretically, and as it is practised in the most ultramontane quarters, it is the dethronement of the Almighty Father and of the Lord Jesus Christ, and the substitution of another sovereign ruler, another Saviour and Redeemer, another object of worship. And the worst of it is that the cultus is vastly increasing in

I

the Roman Church, as her bishops almost with one voice testified in their answers to the enquiries addressed to them by the Pope previous to the assembly of the Vatican Council. Yes, and many of the most influential Roman writers are urging it on, and are contemplating with exulting eagerness the overthrow of heresy and the reign of peace in the approaching age of Mary, when the blessed Virgin will be the almost exclusive object of Christian devotion. In other words, an actual and an appalling— because unperceived—apostacy is in active progress in the Roman communion. The allegiance of men is being transferred from Christ, the Son of God, to one who, most highly honoured as she is, is yet only a human creature. and when the great trial comes, and men will have to deny the faith of Christ or die for it, they will have no faith in Christ to deny, for it will have been obscured and forgotten, or transferred to another.

May God in His infinite mercy open the eyes of these blind votaries of this system of revived heathenism, and restore them to the faith of the Catholic Church, and the worship of the one God, Father, Son, and Holy Spirit.

NOTE.

In all Christian ages the especial glory ascribed to the Virgin mother is purity of heart and life, implied in the term Virgin. Gradually, in the history of the Christian Church, the recognition of this became idolatry. The works of early Christian art curiously exhibit the progress of this perversion. They show how Mariolatry grew up. The first pictures of the early Christian ages

simply represent the woman.   By and by we find out-
lines of the mother and child.   In an after age the Son
is seen sitting on a throne with the mother crowned, but
sitting as yet below Him.   In an age still later, the
crowned mother on a level with the Son.   Later still, th
mother on a throne above the Son.   And lastly, a Romish
picture represents the Eternal Son in wrath about to destroy the earth, and the Virgin intercessor interposing,
pleading by significant attitude her maternal rights and
redeeming the world from His vengeance.   Such was in
fact the progress of Virgin worship: first the woman reverenced for the Son's sake; then the woman reverenced
above the Son and adored.   (Rev. F. W. Robertson, 2nd
Series, p. 267.)

LECTURE VIII.

DIFFERENCES OF DOCTRINE BETWEEN THE CATHOLIC CHURCH AND THE ROMAN CHURCH.

" It was needful for me to write unto you and exhort you that ye should earnestly contend for the faith which was once delivered unto the saints."—Jude 3.

I HAVE given a general exposition of these words in my last lecture. In seeking to make further practical application of them I shall follow the lead of Archbishop Lynch, and as he has been pointing out the difference between the Catholic religion and the Protestant religions, I will ask your attention to some further points of difference between the Catholic religion and the Roman religions.

And first let us consider one of the points upon which the Archbishop dwells in his lecture. He says "Catholics believe that after this life there is a middle state between heaven and hell, where souls not good enough to go to heaven, or bad enough to go to hell, are detained some time that they may be purified from the stains of sin, the guilt of mortal sin being forgiven in this life by true repentance, that they may be pure and holy enough to be engulfed in the infinite sanctity and purity of God. The Protestant says that after death there is only one heaven, or hell, to receive the soul." This is certainly a very mild and limited statement of the Roman doctrine of purgatory. But mild as it is, it differs widely from the Catholic doctrine of the Catholic ages. The catechism of the Council of Trent, which is practically an authoritative document, teaches " that there is a purgatorial fire in which the souls of the pious are tormented for a certain time, in order that an entrance may be open to them into their eternal home, where nothing defiled can enter." Tetzel, an authoritative teacher in his day, rebuked the people (*Just pro sacerd. Serm.* 2, *in* V., *d. Hardt. Hist. Ref.*), saying " Ye hear not your parents and other deceased crying, ' Have mercy, have mercy on me, for we are in the severest pains and torments, from which ye could free us by a slight alms ; and ye will not. Ye permit us to lie in the flames, deferring the glory promised to us.'" And (in Sermon 3, ib.) as the mortal sins of life are almost infinite, they have to endure an infinite punishment in the burning pains of purgatory.

Sir Thomas More, appealing in behalf of private masses for the dead, speaks of the souls in purgatory as suffering pains in fire and torments intolerable, God only knows how long (Works, p. 316). Liguori makes the Blessed Virgin the Queen of this terrible realm. And Faber represents St. Michael as Prince of Purgatory, and our Lady's Regent, the moonlight of Mary's throne lighting up their land of pain. Bellarmine teaches (*De Purgatorio*, lib. II.) that the fire of purgatory is corporeal, that the souls suffering it are sure of salvation, and that they may be aided—their sufferings diminished and shortened by the prayers of the faithful. In the apprehension of the people, the pains of purgatory are identical with the pains of hell, and this is practically taught by such popular manuals of devotion as "The Key to Heaven," authorized by Archbishop Hughes, of New York. The faithful are instructed to pray for the departed, "that they may be delivered from the shades of death, where the light of Thy countenance shineth not. From torments incomparably greater than the bitterest anguish of this life." We are all familiar with the gross popular representations of souls half delivered—with head and arms out of purgatory, while the lower parts of their bodies are being scorched in purgatory. By such representations offerings and payments for masses for the dead are often extorted from the poor. But leaving these popular yet wide-spread notions out of view, let us compare the accredited doctrine of the Roman Church on this subject with the doctrine of the Catholic Church of the first days. That doctrine, as the Archbishop's language implies, and as their authoritative teachers directly assert, is that there are some souls— those of saints and martyrs and exemplary christians— good enough to be received into heaven immediately at death, and that they are so received. 2nd. That there are other souls bad enough to be sent to hell at once, and that they are so sent; while others, the vast majority of ordinary christians, are left in purgatory till they expiate, by sufferings, the temporal punishments due to their sins.

This doctrine is a complete perversion of the primitive doctrine of the intermediate state, and contradicts in explicit terms the statements of the great Catholic doctors of the first ages.

The Catholic Church, in common with the Jewish Church, has always believed in an intermediate state between death and the judgment, in which the soul exists apart from the body—a state of conscious happiness or misery. This state they called in Hebrew, "sheol," in Greek, "Hades," The abode of the blessed in it they described as the Garden of Eden, answering to the Paradise of the New Testament (Luke xxiii.,43). They also spoke of it as being " Under the throne of glory,"—an expression nearly parallel with (Rev. vi., 9) of the souls crying " under the altar" They further spoke of it as being in Abraham's bosom, an expression which our Lord adopts in the parable of Dives and Lazarus (St. Luke xviii. 22). This doctrine is authoritatively proclaimed as true, not only by the fact that our Lord did not correct or reprove those who taught it, but that He adopted it and incorporated it into His own teaching in the parable referred to above and in His promise to the penitent thief, "To-day shalt thou be with Me in paradise." When it is evident at once that paradise does not mean heaven, for after His resurrection he said, " I have *not yet* ascended to My Father."

This teaching was well understood and universally accepted in the Apostolic Church. But it contradicts the present Roman doctrine just as explicitly as it contradicts the popular Protestant misapprehension. Both alike teach that the souls of the righteous and wicked go at once to heaven or hell. The Roman only differs from the Protestant by inventing a third class, of whose existence there is no trace in Holy Scripture or primitive teaching—a vast multitude, neither righteous nor wicked, whom it leaves in purgatory for a longer or shorter time. The earliest Christian teachers explicitly reject both these theories Justin Martyn, A. D. 135 (Dial c. Tripho, 5), says the souls of the pious take up a temporary abode in a better, those of the wicked in a worse place. He stigmatises as heretical the doctrine that souls are received into heaven immediately after death (ib, 80,). He says those who say that immediately after death their souls are taken up to heaven, these are not to be accounted either Christians or Jews.

Irenæus, A. D. 170, (V., 31, p. 331). " That souls go to the place appointed for them by God, and there abide until the resurrection, when they shall receive their bodies and arise in their completeness, that is bodily, as the Lord arose, and shall come to the vision of God."

Tertullian, A. D. 218, states his belief "that the souls of all men go to Hades until the resurrection, and that the soul receives beforehand somewhat of torment or of solace in its prison."—*De Anima.* Origen, 254, says "that the souls of pious Christians go to paradise, which he distinguishes from Hades and identifies with the bosom of Abraham."

He maintains that the perfection of blessedness ensues only after the final judgment. And he declares his belief that *not even the Apostles have received their perfect bliss*; for saints at their departure out of this life do not attain the full reward of their labours, but are awaiting us who still remain on earth." (Hom. VII. in Sev. Nem. II.)

Lactantius, 330, says that " all souls are detained in the same common place of keeping until the time come when the Supreme Judge shall enquire into their good or evil deeds." (Lact., Lib. iiic., 21.

Hilary, A. D. 368, says, " The faithful who depart out of the body are reserved in the safe keeping of the Lord, for an entrance to the kingdom of heaven, being in the meantime placed in Abraham's bosom, whither the wicked cannot enter." (Hil. in Ps. 138).

Ambrose, A. D. 398, says " That while the fulness of time is expected, the souls await the reward which is in store for them. Some pain awaits, others glory. But in the meantime the former are not without trouble, nor are the latter without enjoyment." And so throughout. There is no trace up to this date in any Christian writing that has come down to us of any statement that can give any countenance to the present Roman doctrine of Purgatory It is explicitly taught that none, even of the greatest saints, have yet passed into the final glory of God in the kingdom of heaven. All are in an intermediate condition of conscious happiness or woe awaiting the final consummation, at the resurrection of the body. They know of no saints so distinguished that they passed at once into the heavens ; of .no sinners so reprobate that they were flung at once into hell. And they have never heard of a vast neutral company who are enduring the pains of the purgatorial fire. At least if they knew, they have handed down no trace of their knowledge, and have written much that makes it impossible to believe that any such doctrine was known amongst them.

Many of the early writers were perplexed about the meaning of I. Cor., iii., 11-15. They confessedly can only offer conjectures as to the meaning of the words,

" Saved as by fire." They had no traditional doctrine of purgatory to explain it. Clement of Alex, referring to this passage, says that some will be purified by fire (Strom. vii., 6, p. 851), but it is evident from the whole context that he is speaking of fire even during this present life, the fire of affliction. Origen, on the other hand, thinks that the fire meant is the fire which will consume the world at the last day (Contra, Cels v., 15). And so far from his knowing anything of the Roman doctrine, that Apostles and Martyrs have escaped this fire, and that it is meant only for the middling kind of Christians, he says that no one, not even Paul, or Peter himself, can escape this fire, but that it does not cause any pain to the pure. The same interpretation is given by Basil Gregory Naz. (In Orat. 39, 19, p. 690). Ambrose and Augustin (De Civitate Dei xvi., 24, qq., 25).

In interpreting I. Cor. iii., 11-15, Augustine speaks of the fire of judgment which is to try men's works, and says further, "that they who have the true foundation, even Jesus Christ, shall have their carnal affections and infirmities purged away from them by the fire of tribulation, by the loss of things they love, by persecution, and in the end of the world by the affliction which Anti-Christ should bring." In short, by the troubles of this life. And then he adds, " that some have fancied that after death some further purging by fire was awaiting them who were not fully purified here." This opinion, however, is not an acknowledged truth. It is a mere speculation which had begun to be broached in his day. It has no Scriptural authority. It is not a traditional doctrine of the Church. It is only a speculative conjecture which he will not argue against, since, he says, it may perchance be true. It was in fact an evident novelty in the days of Augustine.

Gregory the Great, A. D., 590-604, may rightly be called the inventor of the doctrine of purgatory. What Augustine mentioned as a private speculation, he lays down as an article of faith, saying, " *De quibusdem levibus culpis esse ante judicium purgatorius ignis credendus est* " (Dial. IV., 39). And yet he does not propound it as a well known traditional doctrine of the Church, but rests his dogmatism upon his own opinion of the meaning of (Matt. xii. 31). He, too, was the first writer who clearly propounded the idea of deliverance from purgatory by intercessory prayer, by masses for the dead, &c. If we compare Gregory's doctrine with the former (more idealistic notions concerning the purifying fire), we may say with Schmidt, the belief in an uninterrupted endeavour after a higher degree of perfection which death itself cannot interrupt, degenerated into a belief in purgatory. The Greek Church to this day has never accepted this doctrine of Roman invention about purgatory.

But what, it will be asked, was the meaning of those prayers for the dead, which certainly date back at least as early as the second century, if the Roman doctrine of purgatory was unknown in those ages? Why, it is asked, were prayers offered for the dead unless they could profit them? And how could they profit them except by delivering from the pains of purgatory, or shortening their duration? If the dead are either saved or lost and no change can now take place in their condition, why pray for them at all? The answer is that the prayers of the Primitive Church for the departed not only do not imply the doctrine of purgatory, but expressly disprove its existence. That doctrine is that the souls of apostles, martyrs, and saints, and especially the soul of the Blessed Virgin, whose assumption is solemnly celebrated,are already in heaven ; that the souls in purgatory are not at rest and in peace, but are tossed and torn with intolerable pains.   But the prayers of the ancient Liturgies are offered for the greatest saints, for apostles and martyrs, yea, for the Blessed Virgin herself, who (according to Roman doctrine) is not only in heaven, but is reigning as Queen of Heaven. Thus in the Clementine Liturgy, "We offer to Thee for all the saints who have pleased Thee from the beginning of the world, the patriarchs, prophets, righteous men, apostles, martyrs."   "The Liturgy, called St. Chrysostom, prays for all departed in the faith, patriarchs, prophets, apostles, and especially for the holy, imaculate, blessed Theotokos and ever Virgin Mary." This alone is sufficient to prove that the Roman doctrine of purgatory was not known when these Liturgies were composed, and is a distinct contradiction of that doctrine. But more than this, many of those who speak of praying for the dead positively declare their firm belief that those for whom they prayed were in peace, rest and blessedness, and, therefore, certainly not in fire and torment.   Thus in ancient Roman Missals were the words, " Remember, O Lord, Thy servants who have gone before us with the sign of faith, *and sleep in the sleep of peace;* to them, O Lord, and to all that are at *rest in Christ* we beseech Thee to grant a place of refreshment, of light and peace."   And so throughout.   None of the ancient prayers for the dead had even an allusion to the pains of purgatory.   There is no petition in them, before the middle of the fourth century, even for the forgiveness of the sins of those prayed for.   They are only offered for those whose sins are already forgiven, and who are at rest in Christ.

After the time of St. Jerome, we meet constantly with prayers that the defilements which the pardoned soul carried with it out of this life may be wiped out, but even then for a long time the pardon asked for has reference, for the most part, to the Judgement Day, as, for instance, this from the Monophysite Liturgy of St. John the Evangelist, "They who have lain down in the grave wait for Thee, and look to Thy life-giving hope.   Awake them, O Lord, in the last day, and may Thy look towards them be tranquil, and in Thy mercy forgive their faults and failings."   By degrees, however, the idea of pardon in the intermediate state for sins of infirmity which were committed here, comes creeping in.   But still those prayed for were held to be already saved, to have had their pardon sealed, and to be in a condition not of torment, but of light, peace and refreshment.

Why, then, were those prayers offered ?   They were a definite realization of the communion of saints, a calling to mind in the presence of God of those whom we have loved and lost, and a tender commending of them to God's loving care, and asking, in confiding love, for a continuance of those very blessings which they were believed already to enjoy.   Much in the spirit in which we pray. "Give us this day our daily bread," even when his present bountiful supply of all our needs gives us every reason to know and trust his loving care for the future.

Again the resurrection and full blessedness of the departed is yet future, and the Ancients prayed for the hastening of the resurrection, much in the spirit of our own burial service, "That it may please Thee to hasten Thy kingdom, that we, with all those departed in the true faith and in the fear of Thy holy name, may have our perfect consummation and bliss both in body and soul in Thy eternal and everlasting kingdom," and of the petition in the Lord's Prayer, "Thy kingdom come." So St. Ambrose prayed for the Emperors Gratian and Valentinian, "That God would raise them up with a speedy resurrection." And so the Liturgies constantly ask a speedy and happy resurrection for those who have died in the Lord.

Another part of these prayers was Eucharistic thanksgiving for the martyrs and for all that had died in the faith and fear of God. And these commemorations were held to be of the greatest importance, as testifying a practical belief in the doctrine of the communion of saints, and that the souls of those who are gone hence are still living, still fellow-heirs of the same glory, and fellow citizens of the same kingdom with ourselves. The conclusion, then, is inevitable that the doctrines of the Ancients concerning the intermediate state was altogether inconsistent with a belief in purgatory, while their prayers for the dead prove conclusively that no such doctrine had yet been heard of when they were written. God has vouchsafed to tell us but very little concerning the state out of the body. The picture in the parable of Dives and Lazarus. The promise contained in the word paradise, Abraham's bosom, under the altar, as descriptions of the abode of those who have died in the Lord. The declaration that they are blessed, that their works do follow them. That when absent from the body, they are present with the Lord. That they sleep in Him as descriptive of their deep, undisturbed rest. This is all the revelation He has given us. No detailed description of what makes up their blessedness, or of what it is to be present with the Lord, or of how that presence makes their sleep in Him far better for them than the most active service of love here. It may be, it problably is the case, that no human speech could convey to our minds any adequate or true conception of what that life out of the body will be. " And the ancient Catholic Church did not strive to be wise above what is written ; she had no traditional doctrines that threw any additional light upon the world beyond the grave." We see distinctly how the doctrine of purgatory grew out of the speculative fancies of later interpreters who tell us that they had nothing to base their conclusions upon but their own conjectures.

It is natural for us to think that that life with the Lord must be one of progressive knowledge and progressive holiness. It seems incredible that we shall not be, even then, transformed from glory to glory by the presence of the Lord. It may, too, be inconceivable, as Dr. Pusey thinks, " that when the soul shall first behold Jesus, and in His sight with its powers quickened, shall behold its past life as a whole, it should not experience intense pain, pain so intense that here soul and body wonld be severed by it." And it may be, as he tells us, an " instinctive feeling that the soul which here has had no longings for God, even if the man himself should be in a state of grace, would not be at once and might not for some long period be admitted to the sight of God." But all we can say is that this is all mere speculation; we are told nothing about it and we can know nothing about it. God would have us commit our dead to Him—and go down to the grave ourselves, trusting absolutely to Him as a Faithful Creator and most merciful Saviour who has redeemed us with His blood and will accomplish His own will in us and for us in ways that we know not of. Even in that last dark hour He requires us to walk by Faith and not by sight.

INDULGENCES.

The Roman doctrine of Indulgences is closely allied to that of Purgatory—and like it is an utter departure from and perversion of primitive practice. In the early ages of the Church the penitential discipline was very severe, and persons were frequently placed under excommunication for long terms of years; sometimes till they were dying and other severe penalties were imposed as tests of repentance and acts of self-discipline. The authority which imposed these censures could, and often did, mitigate or remove them, on being satisfied with the sincerity of the offender's repentance. Out of the perversion of this ecclesiastical discipline, Rome has built up her whole huge system of Indulgences. That system has little or nothing to do with ecclesiastical censures or earthly penalties, but is almost wholly concerned with God's chastisement of sin in the intermediate state of souls between death and the last judgment. They teach that there are two penalties annexed to all sin, Culpa, or eternal punishment; and

Pœna, or temporal punishment, including that of Purgatory. That here, when Culpa has been remitted by absolution, Pœna still remains uncancelled. That one drop of Christ's blood was sufficient for the redemption of the world, while all the rest that he shed, together with the merits and prayers of all the saints over and above what were needed for their own salvation, constitute an inexhaustible treasury or bank, on which the Pope has a right to draw, and to apply the drafts for the relief of the souls in Purgatory. So that any one who obtains an indulgence can apply its merits to himself or transfer them to some one living or dead. An indulgence of a hundred days or seven years means a deliverance from the amount of suffering which would have to be endured during that length of time if the indulgence had not been obtained. A plenary indulgence means the entire remission of all purgatorial chastisements. These are now granted not to persons under ecclesiastical censure, but for the most part to those who are specially devout and obedient. Again, while the limit of human life is less than one hundred years, indulgences are granted, not only for five hundred, but for 11,000, 32,355 and 56,000 years. This system had grown to enormous proportions in the times preceding the Reformation. Indulgences were openly sold, and became one of the fruitful sources of papal revenue. The Roman Catholic princes, alarmed at the progress of Lutheranism, met at Nuremburg in 1523 and addressed a petition to Pope Hadrian VI. for the remedy of one hundred grievances. Among these occur No. 5, " How licence to sin with impunity is granted for money," 67; " How more money than penitence is exacted from

J

sinners," No. 91; "How bishops extort money from the
concubinage of priests. They alleged that the vendors of
bulls of indulgence declare that by means of these pur-
chasable pardons, not only are past and future sins of the
living forgiven, but also those of such as have departed
this life, and are in the purgatory of fire, provided only
something be counted down." They say if any one have
the means of paying, not only are present transgressions
allowed, but permission to transgress with impunity in
the future is secured; out of this they say grow perjury,
murder, adultery, and every atrocious crime. The Pope
to whom this petition was sent implicitly admitted the
truth of these horrible charges. Indeed he could not deny
it, for the book entitled, Taxes of the Sacred Apostolic
Penitentiary, was then and is still extant, with a regular
tariff for the absolution of all kinds of sins, including
simony, murder by a priest, parricide, incest, arson, &c.
This evil had been steadily growing up for centuries, until
it reached its highest pitch under Pope Alexander VI.,
and then the outcry began which ended in the compara-
tive reformation of 1563. But even as reformed the system differs wholly in doctrine and practice from those
primitive ecclesiastical censures out of which it grew.
When it is asserted by Roman Catholic controversialists,
that nothing more is intended by indulgences than the
relaxation of such penances as are enjoined by canonical
discipline, they are involving themselves in the condemnation of the bull exurges of Leo X., June 20th, 1520,
which condems as pestiferous, pernicious and scandalous
those who say that indulgences do not avail for the remission of punishment due to Divine justice for actual sin,

and that they have relation only to the penalties of sacramental satisfaction of man's appointment. It is not necessary to prove by quotations that this system differs wholly from the teaching of the Premitive Church. The whole thing is a novelty. There is no trace of it until A.D. 1084, when Gregory offered remission of sins to all who would take up arms against the emperor Henry IV. The same offer was made to the Crusaders, and it was extended by Innocent III., to all who would take up arms against the Albigenses and other heretics. After that it was offered on all occasions.

The system in its mildest form destroys all true devotion. It transposes the whole religious life into a system of barter and sale. It assumes that no one will even offer prayers to God without being bribed to do so, by a certain fixed tariff of so much direct advantage and profit for so much prayer. It transforms prayer from being the free spontaneous outburst of a loving, trusting heart into a coarse attempt at making a huxtering bargain with Almighty God, until free-will praises and prayers are becoming almost unknown to the bulk of Roman Catholic. Indeed Faber urges, "why should we have any vocal prayers which are not indulgenced ("Growth of Holiness," p. 292), nothing can be more profoundly unspiritual or tend more to destroy the very central idea of the Gospel of Christ as teaching a religion of self sacrifice—of free, glad loving service of God than this whole horrid traffic. For whatever Roman apologists may say, it is a traffic still.

It must be remembered that the practice, encouraged and authorised by the belief of Roman Catholics is, that

the incalculable majority of their own co-religionists, who
are saved at all, pass at once after death into hideous torments of undefined duration—that the sacrifice of the
mass as propitiatory for the sins of the living and the
dead, are the chief means of relieving souls in purgatory—and so masses for the dead are very prominent
features in all Roman Catholic Churches.   Yet, these
masses except on very infrequent occasions, such as All
Souls' day, are not said for the faithful departed in general, but for private individuals, and are paid for according
to a fixed tariff.   The result is that rich people purchase
thousands of these masses to be applied for the repose of
their own souls and those of their kindred and friends,
and so it comes to pass, not only that those who are just
barely capable of being saved, and who, according to
Roman theories, ought to remain longest and suffer most
in purgatory, will find speedy release—while the poor
whose friends cannot afford to pay for masses are left to
suffer on for ages.   And not only so, but the rich by pre-
engaging such vast numbers of masses for themselves,
leave the priests no time to say gratuitous masses for the
poor, however, earnestly they might wish it.   And so
money is made the key of the kingdon of heaven.

"It was authoritatively taught by Troup, of Ancona in
the pontificate of John the XXII., that the Pope as dis-
penser of the merits of Christ could empty purgatory at
one stroke, by his indulgences of all the souls detained
there, on the sole condition that somebody fulfilled the
rules laid down for gaining those indulgences.   He, however, advises the Pope not to do this.   Put the case of
one of the worst kinds of railway accidents, where the

shattered carriages are also on fire, and the sufferers are being slowly burnt as well as crushed and maimed, what would be said if it were to become known that the railway officials had extracted from the wreck only such passengers as seemed able to pay for the attention—and had left all the poor to lie there without help. And yet there is no proportion between the cruelty of such conduct and that of the Roman clergy, if they believe what they say."
—*Littledale.*

One cannot read such things without standing aghast at the boundless cruelty and wickedness of which human nature is capable. Did these men really believe what they taught; that millions upon millions of poor souls were suffering the intolerable pains of Purgatory? That they had the power to release them if they would,—and yet that they could make a traffic out of this agony of human spirits—refusing to lift their hands unless some one would pay them for an exercise of charity, from which not even death should hold them back, if they had one spark, I will not say of Christianity, but of humanity left in them.

One cannot wonder that France has turned her back in scorn upon what she has been taught to regard as the Christian religion, when one reads the accounts of the scandals that have been revealed in the courts of law in connection with this mass traffic. Certain of the Parisian clergy had bound themselves by receiving money for the purpose to say as many as two hundred thousand masses. They found that the work simply could not be got through with, and instead of saying so and returning the money, they arranged with an agent to farm out a large proportion of them to country priests at a lower rate of

pay per mass, so as to leave a margin of profit to the
original contractors, and a commission for the agent. It
was shown in two lawsuits that the agent had not carried
out his part of the engagement, but had simply pocketed
the money (while in other cases the masses had been said
for the barest pittance by starving curates). Imagine the
working of a sytem of religion which thus makes possible
a Glasgow Bank fraud in the spiritual world affecting in
the profoundest way the agonized souls of the departed
and the feelings of their sorrowing kindred ; that it should
be believed that the future condition of souls which Christ
died to ransom should be thus at the mercy of any grasp-
ing priest or swindling commission agent, surpasses all
comprehension.   Indeed this whole system of indulgences
and mass traffic is such a manifest contradiction of the
whole spirit and teaching of the New Testament—such a
perversion of the faith and practice of the Catholic Church,
even for a thousand years of her history ; such an insult
to the reason, and common sense, and moral instincts of
men—that one would suppose that this flagrant departure
from the Catholic religion would be enough to open the
eyes of the most ignorant to the corruptions of Rome and
to set them free from her thraldom.

TRANSUBSTANTIATION

Is another departure from the doctrine of the Catholic
Church. The Roman position is that in the Eucharist,
after the words of consecration, the whole substance of
the bread is converted into the substance of the body of
Christ, and the substance of the wine into the substance

of His Blood, so that the bread and wine no longer remain, but the body and blood of Christ are substituted in their place. This, however, is said to be true only of the substance and not of the accidents. The accidents such as colour, shape, taste size, smell, consistence, weight, etc., all remain unchanged. It is held that the substance which is interior to, and not necessarily dependent upon these external accidents, is that which is converted, and yet that the change is not spiritual but a real miraculous conversion of the substance of the bread and wine into the very body of Christ which was born of the blessed Virgin and crucified on calvary.

It is not pretended that this doctrine was ever formulated before the time of Paschasius Radbertus, about the middle of the ninth century. No teacher before him taught dogmatically that the presence is corporal and carnal. Nay, this position was emphatically denied by many of the greatest of the Fathers. None ever before asserted that after consecration nothing but the body and blood of Christ remained, and that the substance of bread and wine had passed away. It is indeed gravely doubted whether Paschasius ever intended to teach any such doctrine. It is held that what was attributed to him, was the developement of a yet later age.

The definition did not grow out of the statements of Holy Scripture, and it was not a summarizing of a traditional doctrine of the Church. It was suggested by a philosophical speculation of the schoolmen, which is in all probability altogether false. We can conceive of the *res* or *substance* of anything existing apart from one or more of the ordinary accidents of that substance, but we cannot conceive of it existing apart from all of them together. To say that anything is not in any sense what all our senses declare it to be, is to destroy the very bases of all knowledge, and ultimately of all faith too. For if the senses of touch and taste and smell may deceive us, why may not the senses of sight and hearing. And so the *ground* of faith for faith cometh by hearing. To declare, however, concerning anything that it is something more than our senses can take cognizance of, is to transfer it into the very realm of faith, and is in harmony with our experience and observation. As for instance the outward form of plant or tree or animal, and its inner life ; the body which our senses take cognizance of and the indwelling soul and spirit; the mind and the thoughts that dwell in it. That the whole Primitive Church believed in an actual presence of Christ in the Eucharist is beyond dispute. All spoke of feeding on Christ there— eating His body and drinking His blood. But then was t after a spiritual and heavenly manner, or was it a carnal presence that they believed in ? Was it natural or supernatural. Did they teach a carnal eating and drinking of Christ's natural flesh and blood, or did they teach a spiritual manducation ! Did they believe the bread and wine to be literally and actually transmuted into Christ's body and blood, or did they think the bread and wine still to remain bread and wine. Yet to be so identified by the operation of His Spirit in some inscrutable way with His body and blood, as to be called by their name, and to be the instrument of actually conveying them to the believing soul.

No controversy had as yet arisen on this subject. There was no need of caution, and so their language is not marked by the exactness of modern theology. Their feelings inclined them to the mysterious, and so they not infrequently used language which sounded like a belief in transubstantiation or a carnal presence. This would naturally occur where people believed in a real presence, and had not learned the necessity of guarding their words. But then it is evident at once that one clear statement, that the presence was spiritual, or that the substance of bread and wine remained, must outweigh any number of statements that merely sound like a belief in transubstantiation. No Roman Catholic for instance would now say that the bread and wine remain unchanged, and that the feeding is after spiritual and heavenly manner.

St. Cyril, of Jerusalem, A.D. 386, for instance, who uses very strong language about His body being given under the figure of bread, and His blood under the figure of wine, yet says, " That the Jews from their carnal interpretation of His laws were offended at the Lord's saying," John vi., 53. " They not receiving His saying spiritually, being offended, went backward thinking that He invited them to the eating of His flesh."

St. Justin Martyn, 138, in explaining to the heathen the acts and meaning of the Christian religion says, " this food is called by us Eucharist, which no one is allowed to take but he who believes our doctrine to be true, and has been baptized in the laver of regeneration for the remission of sins, and lives as Christ enjoined, *for we take not these as common bread and common drink,* for we are taught that this food which is blessed by the prayer of the word which cometh from Him by conversion of which our flesh and blood are nourished, is the flesh and blood of Him the

Incarnate Jesus." This of course proves that high Eucharistic doctrine prevailed in the days of Justin, but it
proves also that he was no transubstantiationist. He says
that it was still bread, though not common bread; it had
been transformed into a new use. Had he held the doctrine of transubstantiation, he would in all honesty have
had to tell the Emperor that by a miraculous action of
God it had ceased to be bread at all.

Irenæus, A.D. 170 says, " As the bread from the earth
receiving the invocation of God is no longer common
bread, but the Eucharist, consisting of two things, earthly
and heavenly; so also our bodies receiving the Eucharist,
are no longer corruptible, but have hope of eternal life "
(Irenæ Lib. iv., 32). In his apprehension, the substance
of the bread remains as an earthly element still after consecration.

He elsewhere says, " That by the Holy Spirit descend-
ing on the Eucharist, the elements become so the body
and blood of Christ, that though they yet remain figures
or emblems, still the partakers of those emblems obtain
pardon and eternal life." (Irenæus, Frag. 2, p. 20.)

Turtullian, A. D. 218, says Christ called *the bread*,
" His body" (Ad. Judæ. c. 10), and again, bread, by
which He represents His very body (Adv. Marcuis, Let. I.,
c. 1s). Once more, having taken bread and distributed it
to His disciples, He made it His body, by saying, " This
is My body." that is, the figure of His body. But there
would be no figure if there were no true body (Ad. Marc.
Lib. iv, C. 40), he says, "The bread is a figure of Christ's
body by which he is pleased (*representare*) to recall His
body to His followers. In this bread His body is under-

stood (*Censetur*), or accounted. So that our bodies are fed with His body."

Clement of Alex, A. D. 218, says, " In speaking of the Eucharist, Christ showed that what He blessed was wine, by saying to His disciples, " I will not drink of the fruit of the vine, (Lib. ii., C. 2, p. 186).

Origen, A. D. 254, says, in speaking of the Eucharist " Acknowledge that they are figures which are written in the sacred volumes. Thereupon, as spiritual, not carnal, examine and understand what is said. For, as carnal, you receive them, they hurt, not nourish, you. Not only in the Old Testament is there a letter which killeth, but also in the New there is a letter which killeth him which doth not spiritually consider it, for if, according to the letter, you receive this saying, " Except ye eat my flesh and drink my blood, that letter killeth." (In Lent., Hom. vii., p. 5).

St. Cyprian, A. D. 258, arguing against the heretics who were using water in the Holy Communion instead of wine mixed with water (the universal usage of the Primitive Church), says, " That nothing should be done but what Christ did before ; that, therefore, the cup which is offered in commemoration of Him be offered mixed with wine. For whereas Christ says, ' I am the true vine,' the blood of Christ is surely wine, not water, nor čan it appear that in the cup is His blood with which we are redeemed, if wine be absent, by which Christ's blood is represented." (Cyp., Epis. lxiii Cœcilio Fratri, p. 148, Onf.)

St. Athanasius, A. D. 373, quoting John vi., 61-63, says, " Christ distinguished between flesh and spirit, that believing not only what was apparent, but also what was invisible, they might know that what he spake was not carnal, but spiritual.   *   *   He made mention of His ascension into heaven that he might draw them from understanding it corporally, and that they might understand that the flesh he spake of was heavenly food from above, and spiritual nourishment given them by Him." (Athan. in illud Evangel., Op. Tom.   , p. 979.)

St. Cyril of Jerusalem, A.D. 386, says, "The Capharnite heretics were misled by interpreting our Lord carnally, as though He meant a banquet upon flesh, not as He ought to be interpreted, spiritually." (Cyril Cat. Multag. iv. 1.)

Jerome, A.D. 420, who uses very strong language about the real presence of Christ in the Eucharist yet clearly distinguishes between the natural body and blood of Christ and the spiritual body and blood which are eaten and drunken by the faithful.   (Hieron. in Eph. I., v. 7.)

The Epistle to Cæsarius, generally attributed to Chrysostom, says "that before the bread is consecrated we call it bread ; but when it is consecrated it is no longer called bread, but is held worthy to be called the body of the Lord, *yet still the substance of the bread remains.*" (Chrys. ad Cæsarium, Tom. III., p. 743.)

St. Augustine, A.D. 430, says, " Our Lord hesitated not to say, 'This is my body,' when He gave the sign of His body, spiritually understand, what I have spoken to you. You are not to eat that body which you see and drink that blood which they will shed who will crucify Me.   I have commended to you a sacrament, spiritually understood it will quicken you.   Though it must be visibly celebrated, yet it must invisibly be understood."   (Tom.

IV., p. 1066.) What you see is bread and the cup. But as your faith requires, the bread is Christ's body, the cup His blood. How is the bread His body and the wine His blood ? These things, brethren, are therefore called sacraments, because in them one thing is seen another understood. What appears has a bodily form, what is understood has a spiritual fruit. (Tom. V., pt. 1., p. 1103.) "The body and blood of Christ will then be life to each if what is visibly received in the sacrament be in actual verity spiritually eaten, spiritually drunk." (Tom. V. par. I., p. 64.)

Theodoret, A.D. 456, says, "He honoured the visible symbols with the name of His body and blood, not changing the nature, but adding to the nature grace." (Tom. IV., p. 17.) Again, "The mystic symbols depart not after consecration from their own nature, for they remain in the former substance. Though we understand what they have become, and believe and adore, as though they were what they are believed to be." (Ibid. p. 185.)

Pope Gelasius, 496, says, " Certainly the sacrament of the body and blood, which we receive, is a divine thing, on account of which, and through the same, we are made partakers of the divine nature, *and still* the substance or nature of bread and wine does not cease (non desinit), * * * * although by the operation of the divine spirit they may pass over into a divine substance still they continue in the propriety of their own nature (*permanente tamen in suæ proprietate naturæ.*")—*De duobus natur in Christo*, Tom. VIII., p. 730.

And so it went on without any change in the testimony of the Church against the modern doctrine of Rome, certainly till the middle of the ninth century, probably till the middle of the twelfth century.

That all the Christian writers of these first ages use language which teaches in the plainest terms the doctrine of a real (or if it be preferred a true and actual) presence of Christ in the Sacrament of the Altar, is altogether beyond dispute. Indeed they use language again and again which, if such an interpretation were not rendered impossible by such statements as I have quoted, would readily lend themselves to the support of the present Roman doctrine. Those statements make it impossible that such a doctrine could have been held by them. The idea which lies at the basis of most of their strongest statements respecting the Lord's Supper may be said to be this: That as the *Logos* or Word was once united with the flesh, so in the Supper He is now united with the bread and wine; but as the Catholic doctrine has always been that the union of the two natures in Christ was not a transubstantiation or absorption of one nature into the other, but that the two natures continued united in the one person, perfect God and perfect man; so in the Eucharist the two parts the heavenly presence and the earthly elements were united in one Sacrament by the power of the Holy Ghost, yet so that each continues in its own proper nature.

It has been well urged that the Fathers, with all their strong expressions, could not have meant to teach transubstantiation: (1) Because the change is so often compared with that of water in baptism and chrism in consecration; (2) Because it is likened to the union of the *Logos* with the flesh—where there was no transformation of the flesh ; (3) Because the Fathers (many of them) argue against the monophysites, on the ground that as there was in the Lord's Supper no change in the substance of the bread and wine, so there was none in the incarnation ; (4) Because they frequently call the elements after consecration figures and signs, τυποσ αντιτυπα, *figura signum*, terms which no believer in transubstantiation could or would apply to them. And so we may conclude that in this particular again Rome has perverted and destroyed the doctrine of the Primitive Catholic Church, has introduced a degrading materialism into the interpretation of the mysteries of Christ, and has destroyed the very nature of the sacrament by transforming its unfathomable mystery into a mere mechanical miracle.

THE WITHOLDING OF THE CUP.

This is a point in which the Roman Church has confessedly departed from the practice of the Primitive Catholic Church. Cardinal Bona, one of the most distinguished liturgical writers of the Roman communion, says that the faithful always, and in all places, from the first beginning of the Church till the twelfth century, were used to communicate under the species of bread and *wine*. The use of the chalice began little by little to drop away in the beginning of that century, and many bishops forbade it to the people, to avoid the risk of irreverence and spilling (Ro. Liturg. ii. 18). The Council of Constance, which first dared to set aside the Lord's express command, "drink ye all of this," (on June 15th, A.D. 1415, not only admits that Christ Himself administered in both kinds to His disciples, but further declares that in primitive times this sacrament was received in both kinds by the people, and yet in the teeth of an explicit Divine command, and in spite of acknowledged long continued Catholic usage, it decreed that "as the reception of one element was sufficient for the receiving wholly, both the body and blood of Christ, so the Eucharist should be received by the laity in one kind only." (Cl. Con. Sess. xiii.) And it decreed "that if any priest in obedience to Christ's command should disregard its decree, he should be handed over to *the secular* arm, which then meant that he should be burnt at the stake." This is still the unrepealed law of the Roman Church.

It is in direct opposition not only to the plain letter of Holy Scripture, but to the unquestioned practice, as Romanists confess, of the Catholic Church. In Justin Martyn, A.D. 135, the earliest uninspired account of the Eucharist that has come down to us, we read that "the deacons gave to every one that was present to partake of the bread over which thanks had been offered, and of wine mixed with water, and that they carried them also to those not present." (Just. Apol., 1, p. 97.)

St. Cyprian says, "that the deacons offered the cup to those who were present." (Cyp. de Lapsis, p. 64, Fek.)

St. Chrysostom specially notices that there is no difference between priests and laymen in this respect, "whereas under the old covenant, the priests ate some things and laymen others; and it was not lawful for the people to partake of those things of which the priests partook; it is not so now, but one body is placed before all and one cup." (Chrys. Hom. xiv. in I., lib.)

And so onward for centuries. Thus the Council of Clermout, A.D. 1095, decrees, in its xviii. canon, that all

who shall communicate at the altar shall receive the body
and blood in both kinds, unless by way of necessity and
from caution, and this Council was presided over by Pope
Urban II. in person.

Pope Galasius I. says, we have ascertained that certain
persons, having received a portion of the sacred body alone,
abstain from partaking of the chalice of the sacred blood.
Let such persons either receive *the sacrament in its enti-
rety*, or be expelled from the entire sacrament, because the
devision of one and the same mystery *cannot take place
without great sacrilege*. Thus what shocked Pope Galasius was exactly what is seen in every Roman church to-day.
The priest alone receiving the chalice, and the laity abstain-
ing from it (Cup. Jur. Can. Decret, III., ii. 12). So Pope
Paschal II., A.D. 1118, wrote, "Therefore, according to the
same Cyprian, in receiving the Lord's body and blood, let
the Lord's tradition be observed; nor let any departure be
made through human and novel institution, from what
Christ the Master ordained and did. For we know that
the bread was given separately and the wine given separately by the Lord Himself; which custom we therefore
teach, and command to be always observed in Holy
Church, save in the case of infants and very infirm persons, who cannot swallow bread (Op. 535, t. 163, p. 442).

How this is reconcilable on infallibility principles, with
the teaching of the whole line of Popes since the Council
of Constance, and with the practice of the Roman Church
since that time, it is not easy to conjecture. However it
may be explained, it proves conclusively that the Roman
Church in this particular again differs widely both in doctrine and in practice from the Catholic Church.

K

LECTURE IX.

THE CONTINUITY AND CATHOLICITY OF THE CHURCH OF ENGLAND.

"For other foundation can no man lay than that is laid, which is Jesus Christ."—1st CORINTHIANS iii., 11.

THE Church grew out of Christ. It is built upon His person. It is His own appointed instrument for conveying his incarnate life to us. It is the great world-wide and time-long witness to the truth of His history. It was organized and instructed by Him. It began its heroic task of converting the world, at His command, when in the upper chamber at Jerusalem He had shed out upon it His regenerating, illuminating, guiding Spirit. From that centre it spread with noiseless rapidity, creeping on from village to village, from town to town, from land to land, till within a very little while it had reached the uttermost bounds of the West, and had spread to the North, and East, and South, into lands far beyond the bounds of the Roman Empire. It was, as we have seen, called the Catholic Church, because it had this world-embracing mission, and because it was the herald of God's whole truth to man. It did not set itself to subvert or absorb the secular power but to strengthen and establish it by purifying and elevating human life in every land ; and so while it was everywhere one and the same body, in perfect union and communion throughout all its parts, it yet, in subordination to its great central truths and principles, accommodated itself to the political conditions of its surroundings. And so there grew up the national sub-divisions of this one body, such as the Greek, Italian, Spanish, French, and English branches of the one Catholic Church, all subject to the supreme legislative government of the whole body—the General Council.

I have asked your attention to the way in which this original constitution was invaded and overturned, these principles trampled under foot, and these doctrines contradicted and obscured, so that the Roman Church, in so far as she is Roman, has ceased to be Catholic in constitution, in doctrine and in practice.

I ask your attention to as brief a statement as I can make, of the beginning, continuity, and catholicity of the English Church.

Whence, then, came the Church of England ? It is now made clear beyond dispute that the Celtic part of the Island had been almost if not wholly Christianized long before the coming of Augustine in 596, and that Celtic part—including Wales, the kingdom of Strathclyde, and Scotland—embraced quite half of the territory of the whole island. We learn from Tertullian, who wrote about A. D. 208, that districts of Britain inaccessible to the Roman arms—that is the Highlands of the north and west—had been subdued to Christ. A little later, A.D. 239, Origen speaks of Britain as having one religion, and that one the religion of Christ. (Homil. iv., in Eazekl.) Constantius, the father of Constantine, is said by Sozoman to have favoured and supported Christianity in Britain. And Eusebius, the historian, in more than one passage implies the existence of a Christian British Church. There was certainly a large and regularly constituted Church in Britain before the end of the third century, for at the important council held at Arles, in A. D. 314, three British bishops were present, and affixed their signatures to the decrees of that council. St. Athanasius says that the British Church accepted and assented to the faith defined at Nice, A. D. 325. His language leaves no doubt that British bishops were either present in person or afterwards signified their adhesion to the decisions of the Synod of Sardica, 347. Three British bishops were present at the misguided Council of Rimini, 359. St. Chrysostom, writing 367, speaks of the British Isles as possessing churches and altars.

In fact, the evidence of the existence of an organized Church in Britain before the coming of the Roman mission is overwhelming. When Augustine landed, he found a bishop, Luidhart, and his attendant priests, who had come from France with the Christian Queen Bertha to reside in the court of the yet heathen Ethelbert, King of Kent; and about two years after Augustine's arrival we have a detailed account of his interviews with seven British bishops and many learned men from their famous monastry of Bangor. Augustine claimed, among other things, their acknowledgement of himself as Archbishop of England, by virtue of his appointment by the Pope. They replied, " We know of no other obedience except that of love and perfect charity that is due to him whom ye style Pope, nor that he has a claim and right to be Father of Fathers. Further, we are under the jurisdiction of the Bishop of Caer-Leon-upon-Usk, who is under God appointed to oversee us, and to make us keep the spiritual path." Augustine was enraged and threatened, " Since, then, ye refuse to work under my direction for the conversion of the Saxons, ere long, by a just judgment of God, you shall have to suffer from the Saxons the bitter pains of death." And it was not very long till an Anglo-Saxon king, still pagan, marched at the head of his tribe to the very spot where the conference had been held, and, overthrowing the Welsh army, massacred the whole of the monks of Bangor, to the number of 700, and rased their monastery to the ground. " It was a national tradition among the Welsh," says Thierry, " that the chief of the Roman mission had instigated this invasion and pointed out the monastery of Bangor to the Pagans of Northumbria." Be this as it may, the event supplies an additional proof of the existence and extent of the ancient British Church.

But you are, perhaps, asking, Whence came this numerous ancient British Church ? In replying, we may at once dismiss as mere myths the legends about St. Paul, Caracticus, Joseph of Arimathæa, and King Lucius, being founders of the British Church. They have no historical basis. There never was any King Lucius, such as the Roman Catholic legend describes. There can be but little doubt in the mind of any one who will take pains to study the matter that Christianity came into England mainly from Asia Minor through the Greek colonies at

Marseilles and up the Rhone.   During the early Christian
times there was close and continual intercourse between
the Greek colonies of the Lower Rhone, and the Greek
settlements of Asia Minor, of which Ephesus was the
centre.   Greek civilization was extensively diffused in the
interior of south-eastern Gaul.   The Church that flour-
ished at Lyons and Vienne in the second century was
unquestionably Greek in its origin.   The martyrs' names
are Greek.   The first bishops were Greek.   The great
Irenæus, the second bishop, wrote in Greek.   The narra-
tive of the martyrdoms of the Rhone was sent, not to
Rome, but to the Greeks of Asia.   Irenæus took sides
with the Greeks in their disputes with Rome about
Easter and the rebaptization of heretics, and he rebuked
the Roman bishop sharply for his harshness towards the
Asiatics.   We learn from him that the Church at that
time extended not only through this district of the Rhone,
but along the left bank of the Rhine towards the English
Channel.

When persecution broke with such sudden fury upon this
Church, towards the end of the century, thousands were
slain, but thousands fled towards the West, and sought
shelter from their Roman persecutors among their kinsmen amid the forests of the West.   Britain was as yet
free from the persecutor's flail, and as many as could
passed over to their Celtic kinsmen living there, and
hid themselves in the remote districts of the island, carrying with them not only the story of their sufferings, but
the message of their faith, winning many to the religion
of Christ, and thus accounting for Tertullian's saying,
" Et Brittannorum inaccessa Romanis loca Christo vero

subdita sunt," and for the large number of bishops, monks and priests that were found among the Celts at the coming of the Saxons. Bede (B. I. C. 15), describing the horrors of the Saxon invasion, tells us that the priests were everywhere slain before the altars. The prelates and the people, without any respect of persons, were destroyed by fire and sword. Some of the miserable remainder being taken in the mountains, were butchered in heaps; some with sorrowful hearts fled beyond the seas—fled to Ireland, no doubt, as they were being driven to the West by the ferocious Saxons. These became the harbingers of the faith to Ireland, just as their Gælic kinsmen had been nearly two centuries before to England. St. Patrick, who was a Scotchman, seems to have been the first to carry on a successful missionary work in that island. His success, however, was only temporary. The land lapsed into heathenism after his death; and the abiding conversion of that island was accomplished by St. David, St. Gildas, and St. Chadoc, three Welsh saints of the ancient British Church, who went to Ireland at the request of King Anmire, to restore ecclesiastical order, because, as he states in his letters, the Irish had lost the Catholic faith. This Irish Church soon became famous throughout the world for its learning and missionary zeal. During the seventh and early eighth centuries, it was the most influential Church in Christendom. It promised fair at that time to become, instead of Rome, the ecclesiastical centre of the Christian world. From it at an early date went out those famous missionaries, Columba, Aiden, Finnan, Chad and Wilfred, who finally converted the greater part of Saxon England to the faith.

For although Augustine, the Roman missionary, was at
first successful in converting the kingdom of Kent, and
through his agents, Essex, East Anglia and Northumbria, yet when the first Christian kings died, the still
half-heathen masses of the people returned to their old
ways. Christianity, as planted by the Roman missionaries, was everywhere swept away, heathenism everywhere restored, and the final re-conversion of the five
principal kingdoms of the Heptarchy was accomplished
by the Celtic missionaries, who emerged from the already
Christianized kingdom of Strathclyde. Wessex, the last
of the heathen Saxon kingdoms, was converted by an independent mission of the Frankish Gauls, under Birinus.
So that Kent was the only one of the Saxon kingdoms
that really owed its surviving Christianity to the Roman
mission. The English Church, then, owes its origin not to
the Roman Church, as Roman controversialists maintain,
but directly to the Scoto-Irish Church, and ultimately to
the Greek Asiatic Church. This historical record is confirmed by the fact that the British Christians followed the
Ephesene, and not the Latin liturgy, and customs.

The whole Church, then, of England, Ireland and Scotland was one, and the Roman mission had only resulted
in contributing the one small kingdom of Kent to this
final result. Throughout the island, with the exception
of this small corner, the liturgy and customs of the ancient
British Church prevailed. The differences between this
British, or Gallican liturgy, and the Roman of that day
were not important, and there is no evidence of conflict
or hostility between the Churches of British and of
Latin origin. The Roman usage with regard to the time

of keeping Easter was finally accepted as the result, not of constraint, but of an intelligent discussion of the matter, and the liturgical differences were left undisturbed, so that different uses prevailed in different parts of the island, even until the first prayer book of Edward VI. was issued.

But the Church of England itself thus constituted was autocephalous—it had no headship outside itself—it was wholly independent of Rome. It managed its own affairs, and governed itself; and no more thought of submitting its action to the approval of the Pope than does the Church of England of to-day. The claim of the Pope to patriarchal and appellate jurisdiction was not unknown. But it was repudiated. Wilfred, bishop of York, in a quarrel with the Archbishop of Canterbury and the King of Northumbria, was the first Englishman to appeal to Rome. This was a direct violation of the Church principles of that age, for the Patriarch of Rome had jurisdiction only when both parties agreed to refer the cause to him. To appeal from a national English synod, from an English King, and an English Metropolitan, was not to be tolerated by the free spirit which pervaded the land ; and consequently, when Wilfred returned with a Papal decision in his favour, and on the strength of it demanded to be restored to his diocese, a council of clergy and laity was assembled, and unanimously determined that the appeal was a public offence, and the Papal letters an insult to the Crown and nation. Wilfred was condemned and imprisoned for nine months, and became for many years a wandering outcast. By the Archbishop of Canterbury Theodore, the Papal mandate was equally disregarded ;

although the decree declared that all persons, whoever they might be, who should attempt to infringe that decree, should be smitten with an everlasting anathema.

You remember how, at the end of the next century, 790, the English Church, under the guidance of Alcuin, resisted the action of the Church of Rome, and the command of the Pope, and rejected the veneration and service of images, to which they had committed themselves, as things which the Church of God utterly abhors. The claims of Rome were now being constantly pressed, and though they made some progress they were constantly resisted.

In the year 805 the English clergy in synod addressed a letter of remonstrance to Pope Leo on the custom which had been growing up of late of the English Metropolitans being obliged to go to Rome to solicit the pall from the Pope. They pointed out that it was an innovation, and, in consequence, the Pope sends the pall the following year to Wilfred, without requiring his presence at Rome.

For the next hundred years—till the middle of the tenth century—the Danish ravages and final conquest of the land, not only suspend the progress of the Papal power in England, but almost sweep Christianity from the land. During this time, however, the principles of the forgeries of Isidore were being propagated and accepted everywhere in the West; and so, when the Church revived again in England, it was surrounded by a wholly different atmosphere. The whole ideal of the constitution and government of the Church was changed: Papal sovereignty was being enforced. Under the inspiration of Rome, the secular clergy—as the men who were married

and lived in their parishes were called—were being driven
out; clerical celibacy was enforced, and the Benedictine
monks—those eager agents of the Papacy—were being intruded into the places of the parochial clergy everywhere.

The inveterate preference of Edward the Confessor
(1042-1066) for foreigners, and his constant practice of
putting foreign Churchmen into English sees, is well
known.   Increased connection with the continent, where
Rome was already supreme, meant increased subjection to
the Papal claims.   We now, for the first time, hear of bishops going to Rome for consecration or confirmation, and
of the Roman Court claiming at least a veto on the nom-
ination of the English King.

One of the avowed objects of the conquest was to
bring the English Church more completely under the control of the Papal see.   For this end the Pope gave his
sanction and blessing to this robber chieftain, and sent
his legate to assist one of the most ruthless tyrants that
ever lived in trampling the life out of the English
Christians, and in driving English bishops from their sees
to make room for Frenchmen and Italians, who would be
the ready instruments of the Papal will.

And yet the Conqueror claimed and exercised an ecclesiastical supremacy far exceeding that exercised by Henry
VIII.   He would not allow any one of his subjects to receive any actual pontiff of the Roman city as the apostolical pontiff, except by his orders, or to accept his letters
unless they had first been shown to himself.   The Archbishop of Canterbury was not allowed to enjoin or prohibit anything, except it were in accordance with his will

and had first been submitted to him. He asserted his right to stay excommunications, or purely Church censures, and he robbed monastries and churches and shrines in a way that throws Great Hal's sacrileges altogether in the shade. And yet, as he was promoting the extension of the Papal power, he was not so much as remonstrated with by the Supreme Pontiff.

Rufus, his son and successor, went still further. All Church preferments were openly administered for the benefit of the royal revenue. Whenever a prelate or beneficed clerk died, the royal officers at once seized the benefice and held it for the benefit of the crown, until such times as a clerk could be found who would pay to the royal exchequer the price at which the preferment was valued. A system of universal simony was introduced. The see of Canterbury was kept vacant for years, and the king appropriated the revenues. When, at length, Anselm was appointed archbishop, he resisted the king's exactions, and upheld Pope Urban, with whom the king had quarrelled; but it is remarkable that the bishops of England, in the spirit of their ancient independence, advised the archbishop to give up this Urban, who could never be of any advantage to him, and casting away the yoke of servitude and asserting his freedom as becomes an archbishop of Canterbury, be ready to support the king. And it is remarkable, too, that when Anselm fled to the Pope for help, he was kept hanging about the Papal court for years, and could obtain no definite answer to his appeal until the king died. Then came the long quarrel with Henry I. about investiture, which involved the question as to whether the clergy were to be the sub-

jects of the King or of the Pope.   Henry declared in his
quarrel with Anselm, " I will not endure in my kingdom
anyone who is not my subject."   On the appointment of
Ralph as Anselm's successor, the Pope wrote an angry
letter complaining that the see of Rome (which had by
this time, 1114, pretty well established its sovereignty on
the continent) was treated by the English Church and
king with scant reverence.   " No appeals came from England, no questions were referred to Rome for decision.
The English Church presumed to act independently." To
remedy this state of things, he sent Anselm, a nephew of
the late archbishop, as his permanent legate in England.
This was a new and unheard-of claim.   Special legates
had been sent for special purposes, but the establishment
of a permanent legate had never been tolerated.   When
the attempt became known in England, the excitement
was intense and general.   Bishops, abbots and nobles
met in London, and sent an embassy to the King, who
was at the time in Normandy, and the result was that
the Papal legate was forbidden to enter England, and the
Pope acquiesced and withdrew him.

The English Church was tricked by another
Pope into allowing the appointment of such an officer.
The disputes between the Archbishops of York and Canterbury about superiority was referred to the Pope, and
he settled the question by appointing the Archbishop of
Canterbury, who claimed superiority, his permanent legate,
and so making him superior to his brother of York.   It
has been well said that the Archbishops of Canterbury
were thus stripped of their rights and clothed with the
shadow of them.   And still the struggle went on, the

Papacy ever pressing its claims, and the Kings and Church of England struggling against them, and ever and anon resisting and rejecting them. As the result of this struggle, during the next reign the Council of Clarendon was held, and by its decrees no appeal was allowed to be carried beyond the court of the Archbishop of Canterbury, i. e., to Rome, except by the King's special permission. No excommunication or interdict could be published without his sanction. All appointments of bishops were henceforth required to be by election, and every bishop was now obliged to declare himself the liege and subject of the King, not of the Pope.

When John had basely surrendered his crown and kingdom, it was the Church of England, under the leadership of Archbishop Langton, that was chiefly instrumental in extorting from him the Magna Charta, which enacts in its first clause that the Church of England shall be free, and retain all her laws and ancient liberties intact, including the liberty of election. The Pope annulled the great Charter, and excommunicated the Primate and his supporters, and styled John, who went raging through the country, accompanied by bands of cut-throat mercenaries, his beloved son in Christ. But neither Primate, nor Church, nor people would yield to his threats, and the Charter was maintained and our English liberties secured.

The year 1225 is notable in English Church history as having witnessed the first systematic attempt of the Pope to use the benefices of the English Church as a source of revenue for himself and his court. The demand was simply laughed out of court. The king and the bishops were as one, and sent a message back to the Pope that

when other parts of the Church universal had acknowledged its obligation they would not be found lacking.
It was well known to all those present that a similar demand made by the Pope on the Church of France had
just been rejected with indignation.

Through the agency of the friars and the unfaithfulness
of the kings who entered into agreement with Popes as
the readiest way of obtaining the appointment of unworthy persons who were willing to pay him, the English Church was now fearfully oppressed. The Pope
obtruded foreigners into the best livings, claimed the
right to nominate the Primate, and levy taxes upon the
clergy as he pleased. The most valuable livings were kept
vacant for years, and their revenues appropriated, sometimes by the King, sometimes by the Pope. There was
long and determined resistance to these claims on the
part of the English Church, led, at first, by Archbishop
Rich and Bishop Grossetete, who, in 1226, made answer
to a new demand of the Papal legate for money for himself, " We will bear these things no longer. Let him
support you who sent you here without any request from
us." Grossetete went to the Papal Court, and in the
presence of the Pope said, " the cause, the fountain, the
origin of the evils that are crushing the life out of the
Church of England is this Court of Rome, not only because it does not correct these abominations, but because
by its dispensations, provisions and collocations to the
pastoral care, it appoints not pastors but destroyers of
men ; and for the sake of providing a livelihood for one
man hands over thousands of souls to eternal death. It
commits the care of the flock to ravening wolves. * * *

This Court has filled the world with lies, has put to flight all modesty, has taken away all confidence in documents, has lent all boldness to falsifying one's word."

This prolonged and bitter struggle led to the passing of the statutes of Provisors in 1307, which prohibited Papal taxes and appointments; and the statute of Præmunire, 1335, which prohibited appeals to Rome. The National Church, having begun to assert her rights, begins now to review her doctrines, and to discover that just as the rightful legal position of churches had been overborne by Rome, so, too, the purity of primitive doctrine had been grievously obscured and corrupted by the accretions fostered and upheld by Rome, and that in both respects much needed to be done to recover what had been lost. The result of this discovery was the open revolt from the doctrine of the mediæval Church, which took place in England under the leadership of John Wycliffe, during the latter half of the fourteenth century. This struggle was marked by many revolutionary and heretical opinions. The attempt to repress it issued for the first time in England in the burning of heretics; but it went on with varying intensity and success, till the final overthrow of Papal pretensions was reached.

In 1399 the Parliament solemnly enacted "that the Crown of England and the rights of the same have been from all past time so free that neither chief pontiff nor any one else outside the kingdom has any right to interfere in the same." "From the end of the thirteenth century," says Dollinger, "and constantly during the fourteenth they had resisted the encroachments and extortionate demands of the Roman Court, with the united force of King and parliament. And so there are no statutes recognizing the jurisdiction of the Pope or the right of the Pope to appropriate benefices in England, or to levy taxes and imposts, or to appoint officers. These things grew up by custom; but they grew up illegally, either against the provisions, or, at any rate, without the sanction of the law of the land. Ever since the conquest there had been a continuous struggle between the intruding foreign element and the national element, and the men who conducted the final emancipation of the English Church from the Papal power were able to look back over the history of the nation and see that if this foreign influence were removed there could be nothing to hinder the National Church from shaking off the terrible evils under which it had so long been groaning. The opportunity for the complete overthrow of this foreign influence came in the quarrel of Henry VIII. with the Pope. That quarrel grew out of the basest motives, and it was conducted by Henry and the Pope on the basest principles, and was decided on the one hand and the other by purely self-indulgent considerations. The Pope was not the noble and intrepid champion, as Roman Catholics would have us believe, of the sanctity of Christian marriage and the purity of Christian life. The inner history of the negotiations leaves no doubt that he was ready enough to take Henry's freely offered gold and secure his powerful support, and annul the marriage, as other Popes had annulled precisely similar marriages; but he was afraid of the mighty emperor Charles V., who steadily and naturally resisted the divorce of his aunt Catherine. He offered, however, to allow Henry to have

L

two wives, as a way out of the difficulty. With that quarrel we have no concern, except that in the Providence of God it brought the opportunity for the complete emancipation of the Church of England from the thraldom in which she had so long been held.

Her enslavement had been brought about by the agreement of Kings and Popes. For the tyrants of the Norman line discovered before long that it was far easier for them to obtain permission from the Popes than from the English Church, and people to lay hands upon the Church's revenues, and to appoint unworthy favourites to her offices. And so they supported the ever-growing Papal demands, and enforced them as far as they could by fire and faggot upon an independent and resisting Church and people. The cry for deliverance from the indescribable corruption, venality and oppression had been going up for over three centuries, and now in the quarrel of these long-combined powers of evil the opportunity for that deliverance came.

The overthrow of the Papal sovereignty first, and then the rejection of the Papal corruptions of doctrine, was the action of the whole Church and nation ; for the Church and the nation were one and the same thing then. It was not that a new Church sprang up, and overthrew the old, or that the old was abolished, and a new one started in its place. It was the old Catholic Church of England, that had its beginning far behind the days of Augustine, that rose up in its might, and flung off the accretions of ages, and reformed itself upon the model of Holy Scripture and the primitive Catholic Church. Pugin, endorsed by Dr. Newman, says, as quoted by Dr. Carry lately :

"Every great cathedral, every diocese, every abbey was duly represented in that important synod (the convoca tion which renounced the Papal supremacy), and yet the deed is signed, not by the *vox populi*, but by the voice of convocation. The actors are the true and lawful bishops, and the clergy of England. One venerable prelate alone protests, (and yet not against the abolition of Papal supremacy, but against the proposed supremacy of Henry). He is speedily brought to trial and execution; his ac- cusers are Catholics, his judges are Catholics, his execu- tioner is a Catholic, and the bells are ringing for high mass in the steeple of St. Paul's as the aged bishop as- cends the scaffold to receive the martyr's crown."

The act was the act of the ancient Catholic Church of England, lopping off with her own hand that excrescence of Papalism, which in the days of her ignorance and help- lessness she had allowed to grow there, though not with- out protest. No honest man, writes Dr. Carry, denies that infamous things were done in the Reformation period, as well by the fierce bigotry of Mary as by the despotism of Henry. "It was the Catholics," says Pugin, "of Henry VIII.'s time who executed the monks; they did the same to Protestants in Mary's reign; but both executions were in accordance with the decrees of the State and Catholic Parliament." Dr. Carry also quotes Mr. Beard, an ad- vanced Liberal, as saying in his Hibbert lectures, 1883: "We must take some pains to understand a fact which more than any other differentiates the English Reforma- tion. I mean the continuity of the English Church. I speak as a historian, and not as a theologian. It is an obvious historical fact that Parker was the successor of

Augustine, just as clearly as Lanfranc and Becket—Wareham, Cranmer, Pole, Parker; there is no break in the line. * * The succession from the spiritual point of view was most carefully provided for when Parker was consecrated. Not even the most ignorant controversialist now believes in the Nag's Head fable. The canons of the pre-Reformation Church, the statutes of the Plantagenets are binding upon the Church of England to-day. * * There has been no break in the revolution of Church property. It is impossible to fix the point at which the transition " of the Catholic Church into a Protestant one was made (pp. 311 and 12).

The Reformation in England was set going, and carried out on the principle of keeping the continuity of the then existing Church unbroken. Its old office books were retained as the basis of the revised formularies; its ancient orders of ministers, its creeds, its sacraments and sacramental rites, its ceremonies and its canon law, except where they conflict with the new condition of things, remain as they were in Catholic times. There is no trace in the English Statute book of the disestablishment and disendowment of the pre-Reformation Church, and the establishment of a new Protestant one in its stead. There has been no such transfer from that day to this. The continuity was unbroken; there was no Roman Church in England from the beginning of the Reformation until the eleventh year of Elizabeth, (except during the brief reign of Mary, when the English Church submitted again to the Papal yoke.) In that year the Pope excommunicated the Queen, and set up a separate schismatical Roman communion in England; so that the Roman

Church, in addition to its manifold corruptions of doctrine and practice, is a schism and an intrusion, and the Church of England to-day is, beyond all dispute, the ancient Catholic Church of this realm, reformed and restored : and they who have left us to join the Church of Rome, under the persuasion that they were being received into the Catholic Church, have committed the very sin they thought they were renouncing, and have separated from the Catholic Church to become members of a schismatical communion. To bring this truth to the light, to force it upon the recognition of the world, to vindicate it for her own children, and to claim the whole heritage, of faith and order and worship, which belongs to her as the ancient Catholic Church of this land, has been and is the very central aim of what is called the High Church movement. Rome knows it, and hates that movement with a perfect hatred.

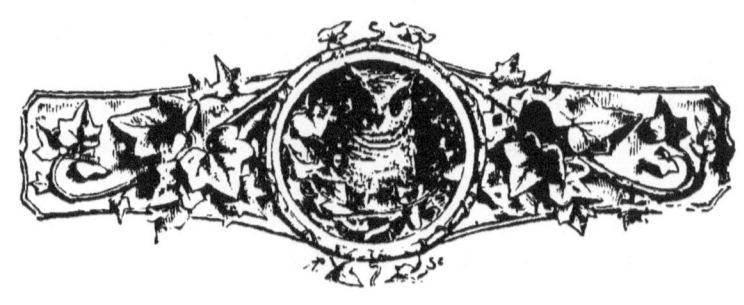

LECTURE X.

" Prove all things ; hold fast that which is good. "—1st Thessalonians, v., 21.

I OCCUPIED your time at great length on Sunday evening last in pointing out the historical proof of the continuity and catholicity of the Church of England. I will be as brief as I can in answering the objections that are urged by Roman Catholics against the validity of that claim. According to the Roman Catholic view, it does not make any difference by whom any national Church was planted. It is all the same—a daughter or branch of the Holy Roman Church, and owes just the same kind of obedience to the Sovereign Pontiff as if it had been planted by Roman missionaries. And according to the Anglo-Catholic view it does not make any difference by whom the Church may have been planted in any nation. It is all the same free from the Church of any other nation, and owes obedience only to the Catholic Church as represented in her General Councils or unvarying practice and profession. And yet one of the grounds upon which Roman controversalists claim the submission of the English

Church to the Roman is that the English Church was founded by Roman missionaries, and is therefore subject to her quite apart from any Divine right which may belong to the Bishop of Rome to rule over all Churches. It is for this reason that I pointed out at considerable length on Sunday last that the English Church owes her origin not to the Roman, but directly to the Scoto-Irish, and ultimately to the Greek Church of Asia Minor, and that she is the direct lineal descendant of that branch of the Catholic Church.

But the Roman controversalist replies, "Whatever you may prove as to your origin, your orders, the succession of your bishops is traceable through Archbishop Theodore to a Roman source; and as the Church in all its parts can only extend and perpetuate itself through the ordination of its ministers, and as the power of ordination has never been exercised by any but bishops in the English Church, therefore the whole Church of England to-day owes its very being to the Roman Church."

The facts upon which this argument is based are these: At the end of the seventh century, about the year 686, the kings of the Saxon Heptarchy, having become Christian, agreed among themselves that the Church of the seven kingdoms should be united under one head, the Archbishop of Canterbury, *as the Church of England.* They selected a clergyman, Wighhard, for the post, and evidently to avoid any jealousy as to which Church should have the precedence in his consecration, they sent him to Rome to be consecrated. He, however, died at Rome before his consecration, and the Bishop of Rome being requested to select some one to take his place, chose

Theodore, of Tarsus, a Greek then residing in Rome.   He
consecrated and sent him him to England. The act was the
result of a particular emergency and a special request—
just as the election and consecration of the last Metropolitan Bishop of Montreal was delegated to the Archbishop
of Canterbury.   No previous Archbishop of Canterbury
had been chosen or consecrated by the Pope, and Dr
Freeman says no succeeding one was so consecrated till
Jumieges, 1050. Under the Greek Theodore the Churches
of the seven separate kingdoms were organized and con-
solidated into the one National Church of England about
the year 690, so that the Church of England is 150 years
older than the State of England.

   "Nowhere," says the historian Freeman, "was the
Church more thoroughly national than in England.   No
foreign interference was tolerated. Thus in the two
councils of Cenwulf, held in the years 797 and 819, it is
put on record that neither the Bishop of Rome nor the
Emperor had any jurisdiction in this realm.   It was this
Theodore who set at defiance the Pope's threat of eternal
anathema if he would not restore Wilfred to York, and
who flatly refused to go as the Pope's representative
to the Second Council of Nice."   But it is said that
Theodore, who himself had received Roman orders, consecrated twenty-two English bishops, and that amongst
these there were several bishops of the Scottish mission
whom he reconsecrated, and that the result of this was to
reconstitute the whole Episcopate of England on the
Roman succession.

   The facts which I have narrated show that it would
not in the least establish the Roman claim or invalidate

our position as an independent National Church if the
facts were as alleged. But they are not. The only
authority for the assertion that he reconsecrated the
British bishops is the statement of Bede with reference
to Chad, that Theodore completed (ordinationem ejus
consummavit) his ordination, and Theodore's own canon,
—that the bishops ordained by the Scots or Britains who
did not conform to the Church of Canterbury in the
matter of Easter and the tonsure, let them be confirmed
(confirmenter) by a second imposition of the hand of a
Catholic bishop. Now, in the first place, there is nothing
whatever said about re-ordination, but only about the
confirmation or completion of an ordination already received.

Then, in the second place, if Theodore did force the
Celtic bishop to submit to re-ordination for the utterly
frivolous reasons mentioned, viz., that they did not cut
their hair in the same way as the Roman bishops and did
not observe Easter on the same day ; if for these reasons
Theodore pronounced their consecration invalid and re-
ordained them, then he was guilty of an act of sacrilege,
and they did not receive their episcopal succession from
his sacrilegious acts, but from their previous perfectly
valid consecration by British bishops, and the succession which they transmitted was the British and not
the Roman succession, in spite of Theodore's action.
But, in addition to this, the rule of the Catholic Church
from the beginning has been that three bishops at least
shall take part in every consecration, not that one has not
always been held to be sufficient to impart valid orders, but
to guard against any possible defect in the consecration.

So important has the Church all along held the proper transmission of orders to be, that she has provided that there shall be three independent sources of this authority in every consecration. At the first remove there are nine, at the second twenty-seven separate sources, from which this consecrating power or succession would come. So that it cannot be broken. It is not a chain, any link of which giving away the whole is gone. It is a net, any defect or break in which only effects the time and place at which it occurs. Or, it is like the weaver's weft and woof. The threads of Apostolic authority are continually crossing and recrossing one another and being woven into the texture of her life. Any broken thread only weakens that particular spot, and is not felt in the web of her onward life.

Now, as Theodore was the only bishop in England that had Roman orders, and as he had to have two other bishops to assist him, it follows that in any case the succeeding consecrations in England, were, to say the least, two-thirds British or Gallican, and only one-third Roman. Besides, the very next Archbishop of Canterbury, Brithwold, was a Saxon, who, because there was no metropolitan in England, and because Wilfred, the opponent of Theodore, who was unpopular with the clergy, would have been chief consecrator had he been consecrated in England, was sent to France for consecration, so that the Roman succession of Theodore would soon run out and a Celtic one from the Gallic Church be introduced in its stead. But the question is one of no importance at all, except as showing on what utterly frivolous grounds the Roman claims to jurisdiction rest, and how utterly foolish are the objections which their controversialists are in the habit of urging against our position.

But the unscrupulous Roman controversialist replies : It does not make any difference what you can prove about the origin and history of the English Church up to the time of the Reformation. The connection of the English Church with the past was utterly cut off, the succession of her bishops, destroyed by the farcical Nag's Head consecration of Archbishop Parker on the accession of Queen Elizabeth. Some of you are probably not familiar with the story.   Mr. Haddan, the great Church historian, who has sifted the whole question through and through, says that the grounds on which this objection rests "are so frivolous and unworthy that an apology is due for condescending to notice them at all.   Any one with the slightest power of weighing historical evidence would be ashamed, if he ex- amined the case, of committing himself to its acceptance." Lingard, the Roman Catholic historian, is candid enough to disown the Nag's Head story. "It was said," he writes, "that Kitchen and Scorey, with Parker and the other bishops-elect, met in a tavern called the Nag's Head, and that Scorey, ordering them to kneel down, placed a Bible on the head of each, and ordered them to rise up bishops. Of this tale, concerning which so much has been written, I can find no trace in any author or document of the reign of Queen Elizabeth."   And when attacked by Roman Catholics for what he had written, he says he " owes it to himself to prove the truth of his statement, and the utter futility of any objection that can be urged against it."

Conrayer, another Roman Catholic writer of note, says

that this fable, which had its birth in the reign of King
James, is not to be found in any of the authors who have
written in Parker's own time. And yet there are Roman
Catholic teachers who repeat this awkward fabrication,
and manifest falsehood again and again as though they
believed it to be true. For instance, on the night of my
second lecture on this subject, a gentleman connected with
this parish was induced by a friend to go with him to St.
Michael's cathedral. The priest who preached apologised
for Archbishop Lynch's absence on account of illness and
said that he had been appointed to take his place and
preach on what would have been his subject. That subject was a continuance of the attack made in his published lecture on the English Church. After a few honied
remarks about his desire to speak with all charity and to
avoid saying anything that would stir up bitterness of
feeling, he set to work and told that whole Nag's Head lie
to that whole mass of ignorant people, as though it were the
solid truth. My friend was altogether unfamiliar with the
subject, and thought that it was rather an awkward fact
in our history.

The facts of the case are as follows: When Mary came
to the throne she either burned or expelled the majority
of the surviving bishops of Henry VIII. and Edward
VI.'s time, and obtruded others ready to submit to the
Pope, and conform to the Roman system. Now, the rule
of the Catholic Church, as expressed in the 18th canon of
the Council of Antioch, and the Apostolical canon 16, has
been that if a bishop be driven from his see by violence,
or by the secular power, he is still the lawful bishop of
that diocese, no matter who may be obtruded into his
place.

It so happened in the Providence of God, that when Mary died, and Elizabeth came to the throne, no less than fifteen dioceses were vacant by death, as the result of the plague that had swept over the land, leaving only ten of Mary's obtruded bishops. These, with only two exceptions, refused to conform, and were deprived of their sees, or rather of the sees of the previously-expelled bishops into which they hed been intruded. Very few, however, of the expelled bishops of Edward's time had survived the persecution and hardships to which they had been exposed in Mary's reign. The See of Canterbury was vacant, and Thomas Parker was chosen to fill the vacant throne in 1559, and four of the expelled bishops who had not yet been restored to their sees, but who, according to Catholic usage, were quite competent to perform the act of consecration validly and canonically, were appointed to consecrate Parker, and they did consecrate him on December 17th, 1559, according to the revised second Ordinal of Edward VI.

Now, all the documents connected with this consecration are duly and fully entered in the registries where they ought to be entered. First, in the State documents, we have duly recorded the Congé-d'Eslire, or instructions to elect; the election itself; the royal assent, with commission to confirm and consecrate; the restitution of temporalities, with the homage. Each of these State documents is duly entered, not only in the Ecclesiastical Register, but properly and previously in the State Rolls. These are two totally independent records of documents the keepers of which have no connection whatever with one another, and which yet so interlace that nothing but genuineness could make them tally.]

Again, the Ecclesiastical Registers themselves, in which
Parker's consecration is duly entered, are kept in different places, at Lambeth, at Canterbury, in the Prerogative Court at London, and all are under different custo-
dians, so that any tampering with the records is impossible. In addition to this, Archbishop Parker, who was a
wonderfully exact and methodical man, gave a series of
manuscripts to his own college, Corpus Christi, Oxford,
and among them copies of the Register of his own consecration, and letters of Lord Burleigh connected with it.
Lingard, the Roman Catholic historian, says : "To this
testimony of the Register what could the champions of
the Nag's Head story oppose ? They had but one resource,
to deny its authenticity : to pronounce it a forgery. But
there was nothing to countenance such a supposition ;
the most experienced eye could not discover in the entry
itself or the form of the characters or colour of the ink,
the slighted vestige of imposture. Moreover, the style
of the instrument, the form of the rite, and the costumes
attributed to the prelates were all in keeping, redolent
of the theology taught in the schools of Strasbourg and
Geneva."

In confirmation of the absolute correctness of these records, we have the letters written by English Reformers
at the time to the Continental Reformers at Zurich, and
only brought to light about forty years ago, which prove
in detail with the conclusiveness of undesigned private
and casual allusions the several English consecrations of
that date, including Parker's. It is also confirmed in the
same unintentional way by Bishop Bonner, a Roman
Catholic, who knew all about it, and who expressly

states that Parker was consecrated by Barlow, Coverdale, Scorey and Hodgkin, the consecrators named in the commission and in the Registries.

Again, Machyn, a contemporary of Parker's, but in no way mixed up in the strife of the times, enters Parker's consecration in his diary, December 17th, as a notable fact, but without the faintest idea of ever making any controversial use of it. Parker, in his own private diary, in words certainly intended for no eye but his own, makes an entry of his own consecration on December 17th. A similar memorandum is made by Parker's son. In fact, the allusions to and confirmations of this transaction found in all sorts of contemporary history and literature, put that fact, if any historical fact can be put, beyond the possibility of doubt.

And yet Roman Catholics who claim to be honest men profess to disbelieve it, and they profess to disbelieve it on the authority of the Nag's Head story. That story is simply as Lingard narrates it: "In the year 1604, that is forty-five years after Parker's consecration, an exiled Anglo-Romanist priest of the name of Holywood, in a controversial book printed at Antwerp, alleged that Parker and some of the other bishops were consecrated (by a mock ceremony) all together at the Nag's Head tavern, by Dr. Scorey, who was himself in turn consecrated in the like mock way by them. Holywood says that he derived this story from the hearsay conversation of a Mr. Neil, who had been Hebrew lecturer in Oxford, but who like himself had been displaced from his post for his religion, in 1569, and who died in 1590, that is fourteen years before Holwood's book was published.

During the twenty years succeeding 1604, every Anglo-Roman writer with suicidal eagerness repeats this story exultingly, although in varying and contradictory forms. Prior to that date Anglo-Romanists had assailed English orders as invalid with an extravagence of assertion quite unrestrained, and upon every ground their imaginations could devise; and yet not only do they who were contemporary with the facts know nothing of Holywood's story, but their objections for the most part turn upon the admitted fact of the actual consecration of our bishops by Edward's Ordinal.

So that this story, which thus rests upon less than nothing, is both in itself absurdly improbable, "to the degree indeed of seriously compromising the common sense of the man who can believe it, and is contradicted by the strongest of evidence to the real facts, evidence indeed of almost every kind possible in the case." (Haddan.)

It bears, too, on the face of it the proof of its falsehood, for it describes Dr. Scorey, the consecrator, as not having been consecrated until after he had consecrated Parker and the others, and then as being consecrated by them on the 9th of September, 1559. Whereas, there is the clearest proof that he had been consecrated regularly eight years before, in 1551. So that we are required to believe that with every cathedral and church in England at their disposal, with a solemn and formal Ordinal which they themselves had revived ready for their use, with four bishops at hand to act upon that Ordinal—ecclesiastics of ability and position, who as bishops showed themselves quite prepared to enforce Church order, and one of whom,

Parker himself, was singularly precise in all matters of form and order—we are required to believe that these men deliberately chose, with literally no imaginary motive whatever to induce them to such a childish piece of insanity, and at a time when they had watchful enemies on all sides eager to find a flaw in their proceedings, to be guilty of a profane farce which would have given them no legal title either to their bishoprics, or to their temporalities, or to their seats in the House of Lords or Convocation, and which would have left every act they did as bishops not only spiritually but legally void; and which, lastly, a Queen like Elizabeth, especially at that critical moment, would not for one instant have tolerated. And yet this is the story which is preached as the truth to an uninstructed mass of people by one who claims to be the chief guardian of the truth in this city!

But, again, it is objected even if Archbishop Parker was regularly and solemnly consecrated, there is no record in the Episcopal Registry of Bishop Barlow's consecration, who was the senior bishop in Parker's consecration; and therefore Barlow was no bishop, and could not have made Parker a bishop.

I reply, in the first place, that if it could be proved that Barlow was never consecrated, it would not in the least invalidate the continuity and succession of the English Church. One validly consecrated bishop is sufficient to confer valid consecration; but, as I have already pointed out, the practice of the Catholic Church has always required three, as a safeguard against any possible defect. Now, in this case there were four consecrators, three of whom were unquestionably consecrated regu-

M

larly, so that the objection is of no practical consequence
But the objection is utterly frivolous. Certainly, all
Barlow's contemporaries, the bishops who knew all about
him, the King, the officers of the State, people of his own
diocese, took him for a properly consecrated bishop.
They necessarily knew the truth, and would have one
and all rejected him had he been obtruded without consecration; and his bitter and watchful enemies, Bonner
and his followers, would also have known, had there
been any flaw, and would have eagerly urged it against
him. But no whisper of objection on this ground is
heard until eighty years after his consecration, A. D.,
1616. At that time it was discovered that the Registrar,
during the Archiepiscopate of Cranmer, had omitted to
register the consecration of Barlow. But it was also discovered that the same Registrar had omitted to enter
eight other consecrations, and several translations of the
same period. It is manifest, too, that this was done out
of sheer carelessness and neglect, by the fact that he
sometimes breaks off an entry in the middle, and in the
middle of an unfinished sentence.

But, besides, this carelessness, is not peculiar to Cranmer's registry. In Archbishop Warham's, just before
and in Pole's, just after Cranmer's, precisely similar
omissions occur; and no one ever doubted the fact of
the consecration of the bishops concerned because no record can now be found of it. The missing record in this
case, it is to be remembered, is solely a record of consecration. We have the record of his confirmation to the
two sees to which he was in rapid succession translated
duly entered. We have the presumptive evidence arising

from notoriety; from the positive law of the Church, which imperatively enjoined consecration; from the law of the land, which required it and inflicted heavy penalties if it was not performed; from the tacit admission of everybody, adversaries and friends alike; from overwhelming motives leading to its performance, and absence of all motives for neglecting it. From, in a word, every possible source from which presumptive evidence can be drawn. Is this evidence to be set aside by inability to find long after a record of it which a particular official ought to have made, but did not—an official who is known to have omitted out of sheer carelessness one out of five of all the entries of the kind? No one now asks for the registry of a bishop's consecration. The known law of the Church requiring every bishop to be consecrated, and the fact that all his contemporaries, who knew all about the matter, accepted his consecration without cavil, would settle the matter for all. And so it was with Barlow. Nothing but plain and positive proof that he was not consecrated could afford any reasonable ground for doubting the fact.

As I have said, however, it is not a vital point, and would not in the least imperil our position if it could be *proved* that Barlow was never consecrated at all. The argument, however, is surely a simply fatal one for Roman Catholics to use. For if, because the registration of a bishop's consecration is not to be found, we are bound to infer that he was not a bishop at all, and that all consecrations in which he took part are null and void; and the whole succession of bishops cut off, then what becomes of the Roman Church? We saw a few Sundays ago that according to the statement of Cardinal Baronius, one of her most learned and devoted theologians, there are fourteen of her Popes in succession of whose election and consecration there is no record, and no scrap of proof whatever, except only that they occupied the Papal See. The Archbishop of Aix says, "that there were fifty Popes at that one time of whom this is true." But further, if the Nag's Head legend were as true, as it is manifestly false, the English bishops of the present day would still have an altogether unimpeachable succession. There are two well constructed loop lines, which carry the succession clear around the point of the fictitious breach.

As I have already remarked, the judgment of the Catholic Church has always been, that one validly consecrated bishop is quite sufficient for a valid consecration. Now, on the 14th December, 1617, George Monteigne was consecrated Bishop of Lincoln by George Abbot, Archbishop of Canterbury; Mark Anthony de Dominis, Archbishop of Spalato; John King, Bishop of London, Lancelot Andrews, of Ely; John Buckridge, of Rochester; and John Overall, Bishop of Lichfield. Now, even if the orders of all the English consecrators of Monteigne were defective, so that they could not validly consecrate him; Yet, the consecration of the Archbishop of Spalatio, made him a true and lawful Bishop of the Catholic Church, and George Monteigne was the chief consecrator of William Laud, afterwards Archbishop of Canterbury; and William Laud consecrated Matthew Wren, March the 8th, 1634, and Matthew Wren consecrated Gilbert Sheldon, on October 18th, 1660, and Gilbert Sheldon consecrated

Henry Compton, on Dec. 6th, 1673, and Henry Compton consecrated William Sancroft, January 27th, 1677, and William Sancroft consecrated John Trelawney, on Nov. 8th, 1685, and John Trelawney consecrated John Potter, on May 15th, 1715, and John Potter consecrated Thomas Herring, on Jan. 15th, 1737, and Thomas Herring consecrated Frederick Cornwallis, Feb. 18th, 1739, and Frederick Cornwallis consecrated John Moore, Feb. 12th, 1775, and John Moore consecrated Charles Maurice Sutton, April 8th, 1792, and Sutton consecrated William Howley, October 3rd, 1813, and William Howley consecrated Charles R. Sumner, Sept. 21st, 1828, and Charles R. Sumner consecrated John Bird Sumner, who became Archbishop of Canterbury, in 1848, so that the Nags Head fiction would have become harmless even, had it been true.

Again the succession of the Irish Church has all along been wholly independent of the English, and is traceable back to St. Patrick, so that had any such breach as is pretended, occurred in the English Church, it would have left the Irish succession intact.

Now, in the year 1618, Christopher Hampton, Archbishop of Armagh, was one of the consecrators of Thomas Morton, as Bishop of Chichester, who was one of the consecrators of John Houson, who was again one of the consecrators of William Laud, Archbishop of Canterbury, whose succession goes on as I have shown above.

The same thing happened in 1684, when Ezekiel, Bishop of Derry was one of the consecrators of Thomas Spratt.

It may be well to remember in connection with the

Irish succession, that at the accession of Queen Elizabeth only two Irish Bishops were deposed, and two others resigned on account of their adherence to Rome. All the rest continued in their sees, and from them all the Bishops and clergy of the Irish Church to this day derive their orders and succession. So that from this standpoint our position is on every ground unassailable.

The other objections that are urged by Roman controversialists against the continuity of the English Church and the due succession of her bishops are either so frivolous or so suicidal that one marvels at their being so much as thought of; as, for instance, that owing to known carelessness of many English clergymen, some of those who have been made bishops may not have been baptized, and that not being Christians they could not by any ceremony be made Christian bishops, an inference which could not, I apprehend, be disputed. But we have seen that there were times in abundance when the worldliness and carelessness and unbelief among the clergy of the Roman obedience was, to say the least of it, just as likely to have led to the neglect of baptism as even in the most careless time amongst ourselves. And besides, if it should have happened at any time in the history of the Church, that some unbaptized man had been made a bishop, it would not, as I have pointed out by the net illustration, or perhaps more accurately by the weft and woof illustration, in the least affect our position now, but only those who lived in the time of the supposed non-Christian bishop.

Again, it is said that our continuity is broken and our orders invalid because we have dropped certain cere-

monies and omitted certain words in the ordination of
priests and the consecration of bishops which were used
in the unreformed Church, such, for instance, as the delivery of the paten and chalice to the priest with the
words, "Receive thou authority to offer sacrifice and to
celebrate mass both for the living and the dead," the investiture with stole and chasuble, the anointing of the
priest's hands, &c. Our answer is that none of these
ceremonies, which are now paraded as essential parts of
ordination, were used in any part of the Catholic Church
for six hundred years, that very few of them were used
for nine hundred years, and that which is regarded as most
essential for twelve hundred years ; and that the ceremonies and words which we have dropped are not used in
the Eastern Church to this very day, though Rome
acknowledges the validity of their orders without hesi-
tation.

If we have no orders because we have desisted from
the use of certain ceremonies and words, then there were
no orders anywhere in the Church at all before the tenth
century, and therefore there can be none now, even in
the Church of Rome itself. It may be taken as certain
that from the beginning the laying on of hands by an
ordainer who was himself rightly ordained for that purpose, accompanied by any words that sufficed to convey
the formal intention of the Church, but not necessarily
everywhere one and the same form of words, has been
held sufficient to a valid ordination, sufficient both as regards matter and form. Authoritative Roman writers,
when they are not writing against us, lay this down as
an unquestioned truth. Thus Morinus (De. sacr. Ordin.,

p. iii., en. vii., 1.) says that the whole Church, Latin, Greek and barbarian, has ever recognized the laying on of hands alone as constituting the essential part (*materiam*) of ordination.   And he says that all the ancient rituals, Latin, Greek, and all the ancient and more recent fathers set forth this alone as the essential of ordination; and to set the matter at rest, as far as Roman Catholics are concerned, Pope Innocent IV. (De Sacram iterandis vel. non c. Presbyter) says, " we find that the Apostles did not use any other form in ordaining, except that they laid their hands upon and prayed over those who were being ordained."   And he lays it down authoritatively that it is sufficient as far as the words go for the ordainer to say, " Be thou a priest," or other words of like force.

There is only one other objection which it is worth while to notice, even for the sake of answering it.   It is said, your orders must be invalid, because from the very first the Roman Church condemned them, and excommunicated the English Church.   The statement is not true, and if it were it would not amount to a row of pins. But there was no condemnation of English orders as invalid for 150 years after, till 1704, and then only in a hesitating way, which cannot be regarded as a judicial decision,   And although the Pope did excommunicate the Queen and the Archbishop, I cannot find that any such excommunication of the English Church has ever been pronounced by the Head of the Roman Church.   I may be mistaken, but it does not make any difference if I am ; for the excommunication of the Pope would not, as the history of the Church makes plain, affect our continuity as a National Catholic Church or cut us off from communion with the Catholic Church. He could exclude neither Churches nor individuals from the communion of the Church universal. He could withdraw his own Church from communion with particular bishops and Churches, and often did so, but this in no wise affected their relations to other bishops or Churches. This was made abundantly evident by the fact that when the Pope excommunicated the African and Asiatic Churches, they not only continued to hold communion with one another, but with all other Churches except the Roman, and they paid no heed to the fulminations of the Roman Bishop except that they answered his excommunication of them by their excommunication of him, and he was compelled to withdraw his sentence without any submission or acknowledgment of wrong on their part.

Again, from 361 to 413, the Patriarch of Antioch and and the Antiochene Church were under sentence of formal excommunication by the Bishop of Rome. During this period the Second General Council was held at Constantinople, and Meletius, the excommunicated Patriarch of Antioch, presided, and the Pope and Roman Church accepted without demur the creed and decrees of that Council. So, again, at the Fourth General Council, held at Ephesus, 431, the Bishop of Alexandria presided, and Leo I. of Rome sent representatives, though the excommunication pronounced by his predecessor Stephen had not been withdrawn. So that we need not concern ourselves about the Pope's excommunication, even if it has been issued. The whole Church as represented in General Council can alone cut off any national Church, or even an individual from the Catholic Church. Parts of the

Church, like the Roman, may withdraw from other parts, but that is all. It does not determine their connection with the whole body.

The conclusion of the matter is that the historical continuity of the English Church of to-day is unbroken from the very times of the Apostles; the succession of her bishops firmly established; the orthodoxy of her faith beyond dispute; and that she stands to-day in this land as the visible, historical representative of the Catholic Church of the first ages, and has a right to claim the adherence and the allegiance of all the Christian people in this realm.

APPENDIX.

HISTORICAL IDENTITY.

THE argument of lectures IX. and X. is not polemical or aggresive, but apologetic and defensive. The Catholic Church, as I have pointed out, starting at Jerusalem on the day of Pentecost, spread from one land to another till it had filled the civilized world and extended into regions far beyond. It was everywhere one and the same body, and yet it was made up of many parts. Each national or provincial church was entrusted with self-government and managed its own affairs—subject only to the control of the whole body—to which an appeal lay from the decision of any of its parts. Each national church was empowered to perpetuate itself from generation to generation, and to extend itself from one province to another. Each such part was a witness to and keeper of the truth in its own sphere, and holding the faith of the whole body, and adhering to its order, was the Catholic Church, of any land in which it might be established. It thus becomes a matter of prime importance to be able to trace the historical continuity of the Church back to the Apostles and to Christ, to show that from their days to these, the one body which they founded has perpetuated itself. Any body claiming for itself the promises, privileges and powers of the Church of Christ, must, as an essential pre-requisite to the validity of its claims, be able to show that it is the identical same body which Christ founded, and upon which He conferred those privileges and powers. This is a question wholly apart from doctrine or from holding the Catholic Faith. It rests upon altogether different considerations, and can only be established by purely historical evidence. It touches the very foundation of the Kingdom of God. A body may possess this qualification of continued existence and identity, as the Roman Church unquestionably does, and yet it may have corrupted the Faith and overturned the order of the original Catholic Church—have so added to and obscured it that it is no longer the same as the Faith once delivered Or a body may hold the Catholic Faith with more or less of exactness, as is the case with many of the Christian bodies that have come into existence in modern times, and yet lacking this historical continuity. This continued existence from the Apostles' time onward it is difficult to see how they can claim as their own the privileges which Christ conferred upon another body which he founded long ages before they came into being. To take an illustration still fresh in the minds of men. To Roger Tichborne certain estates and dignities belonged by the law of succession. He disappeared from view. After some years a man appears on the scene claiming to be the veritable Roger and asserting his right to the estates and dignities. He fails to establish his identity, his claims are disallowed, and the consequences are well known. Another illustration of this principle is supplied in the history of our own land. More than two centuries ago the Hudson's Bay Company was founded by royal charter. It had conferred upon it, whether rightly or wrongly does not effect the illustration, the exclusive right of trapping and trading in all that North-west land. If anyone wanted to share the privileges and profits of that company, it was not enough to call himself a trader, or even a Hudson's Bay trader. He had to seek admission into the company in the prescribed way. He had to become identified with it before he could claim its protection or share its advantages. Another company might be organized on the same model and for the same objects, as was the case with the "North-west Company," but it could not confer upon itself the rights and privileges which the sovereign had conferred upon the original body. It had, after long years of strife and bloodshed, to seek amalgamation with the privileged society before it could secure for itself protection and peace, and the advantages which belonged to the older company.

Perhaps the most easily understood illustration of the principle for which I am contending is supplied by an organization with which a vast number of our Canadian people are familiar. The Orange society has been in existence for some centuries at least. It was established for the purpose of maintaining and extending certain religious and political principles; whether they were right or wrong is another question. It was a regularly organized society, with its officers and members, its badges, its mode of admission, its constituted way of extending itself from one neighbourhood to another. It confers certain privileges upon its members, and aims at accomplishing certain results. No one can become a member of this society except by being admitted in the prescribed way, and no new lodge can be formed, except by initiated members— nor by them without receiving from the parent society a charter or dispensation to organize, and no charter can be granted except by officers appointed by the society to grant it. In this way, this society, which began with one lodge in one place, has extended itself from town to town, and from place to place throughout the English-speaking world. Each national and provincial association manages its own affairs, and is subject only to the rules and government of the whole body. The members of every regularly constituted lodge are received to the same standing and privileges in any lodge in any city or nation, the world over. They are, in fact, one body. But if they had gone to work otherwise than their principles of extension require, and had got up a lodge without any charter or authority from the parent society, then, though they might hold the same principles and aim at the same result as the original society, they yet would not be a part of that society, nor would the members of the new organization be any more members of that society than those are who have never joined the one or the other.

There is a case exactly in point in the history of American Freemasonry. In the old slavery times a certain number of pro-slavery men in the South became dissatisfied with the action or inaction of the Freemasons society in the all-absorbing contest of that time. They accordingly separated from the historical society. They knew all about the principles and rules of Freemasonry. They were refused a charter to form a pro-slavery society, so they determined to form one without a charter. They appointed the same officers, had the same forms and rules of admission and government, badges of membership and of office, and they aimed at the same results. When organized they claimed to be Freemasons, and asked to have their lodges recognized, and their members received as members of the original society. But not a bit of it. They were told that they were in no sense Freemasons, and could only be recognized as such by beginning *de novo*, and by being admitted both as members and lodges just as others who never belonged to any society would have to be admitted. They were only imitators of the masonic society, not parts of it.

Now this same principle must hold true with regard to the Church, which, we have seen by an examination of Holy Scripture, is a visible organized society or kingdom —differing not from other societies of men in its outward form and mode of action—but yet possessing a super-natural life ; by which it is united to Christ—made His Body ; His Bride ; the temple of the Holy Ghost ; the dwelling-place of the Father and the Son. Our Blessed Lord intended the Church which He founded to extend over the whole earth and to last as long as the world stands. (Matt. xvi., 18.) He did not Himself establish it in all places. Nor did His immediate apostles during their lifetime. He accordingly sent them with power to appoint others to carry on their work when they were gone. And he sent them into all the world with instructions to admit new members in a prescribed way by Christian baptism, and gathering them together in congregations, to organize new branches and so extend the society into every place. The history of that society can, without great difficulty be traced either from the beginning down to our own time, or from our time back to the beginning. As a matter of fact though we find that the enemy has always been busy in inciting divisions and schisms; yet there has never been any great difficulty in deciding which was the old Church and which the new. There have been many differences of opinion as to which was the soundest and best, the old Church or the new, but not as to the origin and history of the one or the other. In other words the identity of the body has not been difficult to determine and is not now. That identification, however, carries with it the rights and prerogatives of the Catholic Church though not necessarily the truth of the Catholic faith. Hence the blind madness with which the Roman controversialists have assailed the English Church. Hence the utterly reckless and unscrupulous attempts they have made to disprove her historical continuity with the Church of apostolic times. Hence the fabrications, which though disproved a hundred times, are repeated—as lately in our midst—as though they were unassailable truths. Rome knows that to logical minds this argument is unanswerable. Our Lord founded a Church. It was not an invisible brotherhood, but a visible organized society, with officers, and members, and modes of procedure. To that Church which He founded —and not to any body which other men might found in after times, and call by the same name, He gave certain promises—upon it He conferred certain privileges—over it He appointed certain officers—these officers He invested with certain authority—with it He declared Himself to be intimately and forever united. The conclusion seems unavoidable, to assure ourselves that we are in that body and are partakers of those privileges and promises which He gave to it, and not to another; we must be able to prove that the body to which we belong is a continuation and branch of that Christ-founded and Christ-endowed Church. Rome knows that the historical proof of this continuity is, in our case, beyond dispute. Hence she flies to Nag's Head fables, and with suicidal madness invents tests of continuity which would not only disprove the continuity of the whole Catholic Church for the first thousand years, but would disprove beyond dispute her own continuity, and so defeat the very end she has in view.

This historical identification is not necessarily dependent upon the vexed question of apostolic succession, for if it were even conceded, as those who reject apostolic succession contend, that all power is vested in the whole Church—comes from the people and is conferred by the whole body upon the individual minister, instead of coming from Christ through His appointed ministers to the people. If this were conceded, it would not remove the necessity which rests upon every body of Christians claiming to be the Church of Christ to prove its historical identity with the Church which Christ founded. It would not establish the claim of any body originated by men in modern times, to be invested with the privileges and promises and high prerogatives of that apostolic

N

church. For suppose it true that that body immediately after the death of the apostles, conferred upon presbyters, as is contended, the power to extend and perpetuate the Church, to grant charters for new lodges, to form new congregations, to appoint their officers, and ordain their ministers. Yet by the unhesitating confession of the most learned controversialists who take this view. By the year A.D. 146, this same body had transferred this power to another class of ministers, viz., the bishops, by whom alone it continued to be exercised for twelve hundred years or more, and from whom it was never withdrawn by the action of the whole body. That is the whole body, the original Church, never withdrew this right from her bishops and never conferred it upon presbyters. Those of them who claimed the right to exercise this power took it upon themselves, assumed an office to which the original body did not appoint them, and proceeded to organize a new body without any charter or dispensation or right conferred upon them by the historical church. So that they are new bodies and cannot be historically identified with old, or lay any logically intelligible claim to its privileges.

The only question that can affect the force of this argument of historical identity is this. Does not a change of principles—of doctrines and practices such as took place when the ancient Church of England took on and added to her primitive faith the Roman doctrines and practices, or when again she lopped these off and returned to her primitive condition, do such changes as these destroy the identity of the body? The Church of England was Catholic for a thousand years, she became

Roman in addition to being Catholic for over three hundred years—did the old body cease to be, and a new one take its place when this change was made—or again when she dropped this addition and fell back to her primitive condition did she become a new body, historically separated from what she had been ? Or was she all through the same society, existing under different conditions and with different aims and modes of action for the time being ? Let us see how other societies and organizations are affected by similar changes of principle and of action. Take the two great political parties of England, the Whigs and Tories. It is well known that they have both completely changed, in fact exactly reversed their principles and line of action in regard to their foreign policy, the Tories first fiercly opposing all interference on the part of England in foreign politics and affairs, and the Whigs maintaining her duty to do so, and to make her influence felt especially on the continent; and then each of these parties wheeling right about and adopting the precisely opposite policy to that which they had pursued before. Did the Conservative party or the Whig lose its historical continuity and existence by this change ? Clearly not. The great central line of policy was retained by each, and though in this particular the change was great, the identity of each was retained ? So the Church of England through all the changes above described, great though they were, held the great central doctrines and practices of the Catholic Church unchanged and remained the identical same body through all.

The history of the Jewish Church supplies a striking, and to my mind a conclusive analogy on this point. That church became very corrupt at several periods in its history, but it did not therefore cease to be God's covenant people and church. Thus in the reign of King Ahaz, B.C. 728, the idolatrous religion of Syrians was introduced even into Jerusalem itself. Altars were erected to the Syrian gods or idols. The temple itself was altered in many respects according to a Syrian model, and finally it was shut up entirely (Jahn's Heb. Commonwealth, B.k.V. 41). Again Manasseh, B.C. 644, upheld idolatry by all the influence of regal powers, erected idolatrous altars even within the Temple itself, set up an image which was worshipped with obscene rites, maintained a herd of necromancers, astrologers, soothsayers of various kinds, and even sacrificed his own son to the idol Moloch (2 Kings, xxii. 11). Again it appears that at the beginning of the reign of Josiah, B.C. 611, the book of the law of the Lord—that is the Scriptures—was almost wholly forgotten, and its contents unknown, even Hilkiah, the High Priest, knew almost nothing of it. And yet the Jewish Church was not destroyed or set aside, and a new church established in its stead. It was called to reformation, and was again and again restored in spite of its terrible ignorance and unfaithfulness and sin, and from this we are surely taught that though such sins in God's people and by his church are very terrible sins, and will be sorely punished, yet nothing but a deliberate apostacy, a renunciation of faith in Christ and communion with His people could destroy His church or cause any national branch of it to terminate and cease to be. A man may be desperately sick, the whole body filled with wounds and bruises and putrifying sores, but he is the same man still that he was when well, and he will be the same if he recovers from his sickness. A man who was once upright and honest and religious may fall into most degrading and debasing sins, but fallen though he be, he is the same man as before and he will be the same if through the grace of God he recovers himself and reforms his life and character. So with the Church of England through all the changes of outward circumstance of sentiment and of spiritual condition, she has continued to be the identical same body—the one true Catholic and apostolic church of this realm.

INDEX.

LECTURE IV.

LECTURE V.

LECTURE VI.

LECTURE VII.